Policy Deployment & Lean Implementation Planning

10 Step Roadmap to Successful Policy Deployment Using Lean as a System

DEVELOPMENT WORKBOOK

VINCE FAYAD AND LARRY RUBRICH

WCM Associates LLC
Fort Wayne, IN
www.wcmfg.com

Policy Deployment & Lean Implementation Planning

10 Step Roadmap to Successful Policy Deployment Using Lean as a System

By
Vince Fayad and Larry Rubrich

Copyright 2009 Vince Fayad and Larry Rubrich
Second Printing 2011, revised
All rights reserved.
Printed in the United States of America

No part of this book may be reproduced or utilized in any form or by any means, electronic or mechanical, including photocopying, recording, or by any information storage and retrieval system, without the permission of the publisher. Address all inquiries to:

WCM Associates LLC
834 Mill Lake Road
Fort Wayne, IN 46845
260-637-8064
Fax: 260-637-2284
www.wcmfg.com

Disclaimer

Demonstrations and illustrations contained herein provide only a description of general improvement techniques and methods. Illustrations and directions may not provide all necessary or relevant information and the authors suggest that you refer to appropriate equipment manuals specific to the particular task or contact a qualified craftsman or professional. By purchasing this book and not immediately returning it after reviewing this disclaimer, you agree that the authors may not be held responsible for any omissions or inaccuracies in any information provided herein.

ISBN # 978-0-9793331-2-5

Front and rear cover design by:
Robert Aulicino
928-708-9445

Book and text design by WCM Associates LLC
Printed and bound by:
Thomson-Shore, Inc.
Dexter, MI
734-426-3939

Library of Congress Catalog Card Number: 2009924582

Dedication

Vince Fayad

I would like to dedicate this workbook to Bob Ayers, my professional mentor, who always got upset with me whenever I suggested he was "one of the best bosses I ever had," and to Larry Rubrich and the WCM Associates organization whose professionalism and commitment to Lean made this workbook possible, and finally to my family (Chris, Lanner, Tercel, and Kate) who have been very tolerant of my workaholic lifestyle—love ya all and make it a great day!

Larry Rubrich

To Vince Fayad, whose simple, yet extremely powerful 10-step process gives all organizations an opportunity to close the loop between their business goals and Lean. A groundbreaking process!

To Mattie Watson, whose suggestions and ideas make this book an easier read.

To my daughter, Kelly, page layout, editor, and publisher extraordinaire, who does a wonderful job in spite of my constant pressure.

To my loving wife, Shirley, who has supported me in my passion for Lean.

Table of Contents

Introduction, 1

PART I: Lean Overview, 11

Lean Planning, 14

Lean Concepts, 23

Lean Tools, 27

Lean Culture, 51

    Leadership, 59
    Communication, 68
    Empowerment, 72
    Teamwork, 73

PART II: 10 Steps to Successful Policy Deployment

Step 1: Establish a Mission and Guiding Principles, 79

Step 2: Develop Business Goals, 101

Step 3: Brainstorm for Opportunities to Achieve Goals, 111

Step 4: Define Parameters to Value Opportunities, 121

Step 5: Establish Weighting Requirements, Rate Opportunities, & Prioritize, 127

Step 6: Conduct a Reality Check, 137

Step 7: Develop Lean Implementation Plan, 143

Step 8: Develop Bowling Chart, 157

Step 9: Countermeasures, 169

Step 10: Conducting Monthly Business Reviews, 191

Conclusion/Summary, 201

Appendix A—Advanced Lean Tools, 205

Index, 211

Introduction

This book is intended for organizations that are either just starting their Lean journey or are unhappy with the results of their Lean implementation so far.

Organizations that have used Lean to become a World Class Enterprise and remain globally competitive use Lean as a "system" to achieve the organization's goals. They understand that, for organizations to successfully achieve their goals, Policy Deployment must be used to deploy these goals throughout all parts of the organization. Lean is then used as the "system" for achieving the required improvements as stated in the organizational goals part of Policy Deployment.

Unfortunately, the number of organizations that have been successful in achieving their goals and moving toward World Class performance using Lean is small. The annual Industry Week Census of Manufacturers (released in October of 2007) reported that 70% of the manufacturing plants responding to the survey replied that they were using Lean as an improvement method. When asked about their progress toward becoming World Class, the responses were as follows:

√ Introduction

- No Progress to Some Progress—74% (this number has not changed significantly over the years)

- Significant Progress—24%

- Fully Achieved (World Class Status)—2%

Since we would contend that Lean in the hands of an organization's associates can make any required improvement or solve any business problem, why are 74% of organizations using Lean showing "no" or "some" progress, when properly implemented Lean activities can show "significant progress" in the first year? The answer is that business organizations are not "closing the loop" between their business strategies, plans, budgets, and Lean as the system to make the plans a reality. When these businesses are asked how they are performing against their plans or budget, the answer is often, "This is what we hope to achieve." As Vince would say, "Hope is not a strategy!"

For most organizations, Lean is an add-on, an appendage. These businesses are not using Lean as a way of running their business. They are not closing the loop between required goals and required results and therefore Lean is underutilized as a business improvement process. See Figure #1.

In Larry Rubrich's book, *How to Prevent Lean Implementation Failures—10 Reasons Why Failures Occur*, the eighth reason expressed is: "People Measures/Goals Which Are Not Aligned With Implementation Goals". The importance of tying the company goals into Lean activities

Organization's Lean Implementation Scenario	What Lean Looks Like in the Organization	Amount of Progress
Limited or No Top Down Management Leadership and Support	Using the Lean Tools Only – Random Kaizen Events – Lean is an Appendage	None to Some
Full Top Down Management Leadership and Support	An Organized Use of the Tools and Kaizen Events – Communication Improved, Teams Used	Significant Progress
Policy Deployment with Lean Used as the System to Achieve the Organization's Goals	Every Associate in the Organization is Involved and Participating in Using Lean to Help the Company Achieve its Goals	Fully Achieved

Figure #1
Lean's Potential Versus How It Is Implemented

must be emphasized. Every organization has hundreds of problems, and all of them cannot be fixed at once. So the emphasis should be on making sure all Lean activities are focused on fixing the problems that will help the organization achieve its current weekly, monthly, annual, and long-term strategic goals. Solving business problems not currently in the "plan" will put the company in the "no" or "some" progress category as mentioned above.

The goal of this book is to provide the reader with a proven 10-step process that will take the organization's policies and goals (as developed by the top leaders and

√ Introduction

managers), and develop and deploy a Lean implementation plan to achieve these goals using the resources of the entire organization. Several things to note:

- If the organization has not developed a mission, vision, and guiding principles of behavior statements, these must be developed during the process

- If the organization has not developed organizational goals, goal creation will become part of this process

- It is assumed that all the human resources within the company are available to support this process and that goals and implementation plans other than the ones created in this process will not exist

- This process could replace the budgeting and planning processes in some businesses, especially those companies that develop budgets which involve only a handful of people and not the entire system

Since resource availability is always an issue the first time this process is completed (since we are doing our normal fire fighting and now fire prevention simultaneously), here are some guidelines for each step to use.

Steps 1 & 2 = Leadership Team

Step 3 = Supervisors/Middle Managers & Leadership Team

Steps 4 through 6 = Leadership Team

Steps 7 & 8 = Supervisors/Middle Managers & Leadership Team

Step 9 = Leadership Team

Step 10 = Supervisors/Middle Managers & Leadership Team

Understand that except for Steps 1 and 2, where generally only the Leadership Team has the vision and knowledge of where the organization should be going and what it needs to achieve, these resources are minimums. Leaving the supervisors and managers out of any of the noted Steps is fatal to this process. Their ideas, involvement, participation, ownership, and accountability, as well as that of their associates, is vital to this process.

This book refers to these groups as the Leadership Team and the "team." The "team" includes the Leadership Team and any additional resources that have been included in the process or steps. A typical Leadership Team includes the CEO, President, General Manager, or Plant Manager (the top ranking manager in a facility) and their staffs.

Before starting this process, it is important to note some of the roadblocks, barriers, and process delays that can occur in the completion of these 10 Steps.

The lack of Lean "system thinking" is one of them. We broadly define the system as the processes required from the time the customer places the order for a product or service until the service is performed or the product ships and the cash is received. For customer satisfaction to occur, everyone in the organization must have "system thinking" as a common goal so they all

---

10 STEPS TO SUCCESSFUL POLICY DEPLOYMENT

1. Establish a Mission and Guiding Principles
2. Develop Business Goals
3. Brainstorm for Opportunities to Achieve Goals
4. Define Parameters to Value Opportunities
5. Establish Weighting Requirements, Rate Opportunities, and Prioritize
6. Conduct a Reality Check
7. Develop Lean Implementation Plan
8. Develop Bowling Chart
9. Countermeasures
10. Conducting Business Reviews

will pull in the same direction (a common goal is one of the four requirements for teamwork to occur). System thinking requires that all decisions and improvements in an organization are made based on their impact on the "system efficiency." If a suggested improvement will improve department efficiency but will negatively impact the system efficiency, it is not done. For example, a typical accounting department will run company checks once per week because of the setup/changeover time involved in the process. While this is more efficient for the accounting department, how does it serve the rest of the system, including suppliers? As another example, often a production control department will batch run many manufacturing work orders (see Figure #2) because of the setup/preparation time for the process. Remember, waste is created any time the flow stops.

**Figure #2
Batched Manufacturing Work Orders**

Many companies have used Lean/World Class Manufacturing techniques to make their production areas more competitive and improve customer satisfaction, yet these same companies often still find themselves falling short of being able to compete globally, and therefore consider chasing the low wages of a foreign country. Why are these companies having trouble competing globally? The answer to this question is that the costs that end up in the selling prices of our products are not just manufacturing costs; they are the costs of the entire Enterprise. To compete globally, we need a Lean Enterprise. The reasons we have not applied Lean to the entire Enterprise are noted below.

First, we have defined "adding value," an absolutely critical measure in Lean, in manufacturing terms. It is defined as "changing the shape or form of the product" or as "what the customer is willing to pay for." These both have manufacturing connotations. This is supported by the fact that many Value Stream Mapping books only consider the manufacturing operations when calculating the percent of value-added time. What about the cost (and impact on our lead times) of the ten days the customer order spent in the administrative/engineering areas before it hit the shop floor?

Secondly, this manufacturing definition of adding value has led us to ignore the administrative function and its impact on overhead costs. Yet, can we produce a physical product in manufacturing without the "knowledge product" or "information product" known as the engineering drawing? Or without the customer order entered into our system, or without raw materials? Or could we produce a quality product without standard work?

Introduction

The administrative areas of our companies do produce a product—not like the physical product we produce in manufacturing, but a knowledge or information product that supports the production of the physical product. Unfortunately, our Lean concentration in manufacturing and our lack of understanding of what products are produced in our office areas, have left us with administrative areas that are the least productive areas of our companies.

Why are administrative areas the least productive part of our business? One reason: we don't do something in our administrative areas that we always do in manufacturing—measure! We know how many widgets all of our machines can produce in an hour, and how many widgets we can assemble and ship in a day, but we don't know how many information/knowledge products (quotes, customer orders, new designs, work orders, part purchases, etc.) we can do in an hour or a day.

Once the administrative functions understand that they are in production also, there is one other roadblock/barrier to system thinking. Administrative departmentalization! Companies have known for many years that the cellurization of our manufacturing processes (grouping machines by product or family of products rather than by function) makes them significantly more efficient, yet we have almost no cellurization in our administrative areas. Departmentalization roadblocks businesses from achieving the Lean Enterprise because:

- Departmentalization usually means individual departmental goals. Individual department goals prevents teamwork throughout the organization, since everyone is most concerned about achieving their own department's goals and how that will impact their own performance reviews and merit pay increases.

♦ Individual department goals reduce the system efficiency because they allow individuals within a department to make bad decisions. For example, people working for a department (instead of the system) generally process the "information product" passing through their department in production batches. They use batch production because for their department, batching is most efficient (due to mental or physical setup time). Unfortunately, batching stops the information product flow, extending the information product lead-time, and making the system less efficient. Additionally, these individual department goals may cause other behaviors detrimental to system efficiency: for example, the salesperson who cares only about "getting the order" and not making sure that all the required information to produce the order is obtained, or engineering tossing a product design "over the wall" to manufacturing even though the design is not production ready.

♦ Departmentalization inhibits cross-training, which prevents associate growth. It limits the full utilization of our mental resources in improving the system efficiency since few people understand how the system operates.

Start Planning and Creating the Lean Enterprise Today!

It should be noted that the details in this book of how we use Policy Deployment are different than how the Japanese use Hoshin Kanri. The Japanese version of Policy Deployment is sophisticated and people resource intensive. In a recent discussion with a large corporation that was implementing Hoshin Kanri under the guidance of a Japanese trained US Consulting company, it was noted that they had to hire two people to help administer the process. That said, it is a powerful and appropriate tool for large organizations. For companies of 500 people or less, who often do not have formal goals, and whose operating budgets were created by two or three people, it is less appropriate and therefore generally not used.

The 10 Steps laid out in this book take the average management group, led by a trained facilitator, four or five days of hard work. Then the daily, weekly, and monthly follow-up by all members of the organization begins. It is a culture changing process that will make Lean the system by which the company is run.

Lean Overview

We begin our discussion of how to successfully implement Lean as a system with an overview of Lean and identifying the four basic components of Lean:

- Lean Planning
- Lean Concepts
- Lean Tools
- Lean Culture

It is important to note that the order of component discussion may seem incorrect/out of order to current Lean practitioners. The tendency is to jump to the *Lean Tools* first. While this can result in "some progress," the road to using Lean as a system and becoming World Class starts with the end in mind—*Lean Planning*. Before an organization can become truly successful with Lean, it must understand and commit to why it is implementing Lean—to create a safe and profitable organization.

The commitment to *Lean Planning* ensures Lean will not be used as an appendage in the organization, but as a system to accomplish the #1 objective, the organization's goals. To do otherwise reduces an organization's opportunity to fully utilize the power of Lean (Figure #1).

All four of these components must be implemented to their fullest extent throughout the organization, in a timely manner, to be successful. Most organizations like to pick and choose which elements of Lean they would like to implement, primarily because they do not understand that Lean is a total system and represents a complete and comprehensive culture change in their organization. Lean represents a completely new way of managing the organization.

To be successful, a company must be in balance. It must achieve the correct balance when it comes to using *Lean Planning*, understanding *Lean Concepts*, using the correct *Lean Tools*, and empowering its workforce by creating a *Lean Culture* (See Figure #3). All four components must be in place to have a truly Lean Organization and to have the makings of a World Class Enterprise.

There are numerous organizations in the United States that have either failed in their attempts to implement Lean or have not tapped into the full 100% potential of what a system like Lean has to offer. Most Americans do not seem to understand the significance of creating a culture that is conducive to Lean by empowering the workforce. We do not truly understand the concepts of Lean and the importance of looking at and improving the total system. Most importantly, we do not grasp the concept that Lean must be linked to the business objectives of an organization and the planning required to meet those objectives.

Many organizations try to implement some of the *Lean Tools*, such as 5S, Value Stream Mapping, Problem Solving, Error Proofing, Process Cells, Kanbans, etc., and think they are implementing Lean. Wrong!

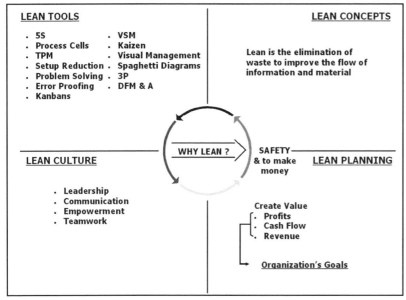

Figure #3
The Four Components of Lean

We like to apply certain tools that Lean has to offer because we tend to be action oriented. We are doers and like to see things getting done. We do not like to deal with people issues. We do not necessarily take the time to really understand the principles of Lean or are afraid of the drastic changes these principles represent. But most importantly, we do not understand the power of planning. We are notorious for the ready, fire, aim concept.

To be successful, an organization must develop a plan that incorporates the Lean tools and concepts and then empower its people to make it happen! The Leadership Team must understand that the deployment of the four components of Lean cannot and must not be thought of as being implemented sequentially (*Lean Planning, Lean Concepts, Lean Tools, and Lean Culture*). These components must be thought of as being institutionalized in a parallel fashion. It is up to the Leadership Team to thoroughly understand all four components and figure out the best possible scenario that best fits the organization.

There is no magic wand. There is no magic formula for change. In this respect, every organization is different. The plan for one organization may be and should be different from the next organization. What works in one organization may not work in another organization. That is why we call it a Leadership Team. This is a led process. It is up to the Leadership Team to know, understand, and properly deploy the four components of Lean to successfully achieve the vision of the organization.

Lean Planning

Lean creates value for your organization. If you are a not-for-profit organization, creating value may be measured in how many people your organization is able to help with available funds. The more money you spend on wasted activities, the fewer people you will be able to help.

If you are a for-profit organization, creating value is measured in terms of the organization's ability to make money. This is normally measured as Operating Income, Earnings Before Interest, Taxes, Depreciation, and Amortization (EBITDA), or Net Income, although some organizations say that measuring Return on Invested Capital (ROIC) and Economic Value Added (EVA) are better measures of creating value. Regardless of how it is measured or reported, the significance is the same; if you are not making money you will go out of business or you will be getting a lot of "adult help" from some corporate office.

Cash Flow is important whether you are a not-for-profit or a for-profit organization. If you do not have money to make payroll, you either have to borrow money or go out of business. Borrowing money is expensive and creates no value for your organization. Going out of business should not be an option.

==Revenue growth should only be considered once the organization is profitable and has good cash flow. Why would any organization have a growth strategy if it is not currently profitable? Many companies think they would be more profitable if they had more business. Once again, wrong! Size the organization and get it profitable and then consistently grow the business profitably.==

This book is designed to help any organization, whether it is a not-for-profit or a for-profit organization, achieve the business objectives of the organization by using *Lean Planning*, understanding *Lean Concepts*, using *Lean Tools*, and empowering its workforce by creating a *Lean Culture*. As the discussion on Lean Planning continues, it will be related to the Policy Deployment process by noting which step in the process it refers to. Steps are covered in detail in the next chapter.

One of the first activities in implementing Lean is for the Leadership Team to establish high level goals for the organization (Step 2 in the Policy Deployment process after establishing a mission and guiding principles). These goals should focus on the business and strategic objectives and should be stated in the same format as the following examples:

10 STEPS TO SUCCESSFUL POLICY DEPLOYMENT

1. Establish a Mission and Guiding Principles

2. Develop Business Goals

3. Brainstorm for Opportunities to Achieve Goals

4. Define Parameters to Value Opportunities

5. Establish Weighting Requirements, Rate Opportunities, and Prioritize

6. Conduct a Reality Check

7. Develop Lean Implementation Plan

8. Develop Bowling Chart

9. Countermeasures

10. Conducting Business Reviews

√ Lean Overview

- We will improve our operating income from 8% to 12% in the next 12 months

- We will increase the number of people we provide care for from 80 to 120 with the same resources within the next 18 months

- We will improve our inventory turns from 6 to 10 over the next 12 months

- We will grow our business through new products and services from $40M to $50M over the next 24 months

The Leadership Team must limit the number of goals. It is recommended that three to five goals be established. Once the number of goals gets beyond five, people do not remember them and no longer use them to guide their decision-making processes. Remember, three to five goals only!

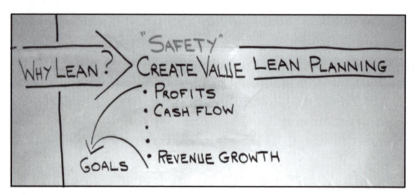

**Figure #4
Lean Planning Component**

One of the goals must always be SAFETY. The only thing that takes precedence over business objectives is safety. The goal for safety must always be zero incidents. Note that for the many companies that are already reporting

16

some "lost injury" (lost time) days, their initial goal should be zero lost injury days. All identifiable safety issues must be dealt with immediately. All World Class Enterprises (WCE) have a clear policy statement that effectively communicates that the company will "provide a safe, clean, neat, and organized working environment" for all associates.

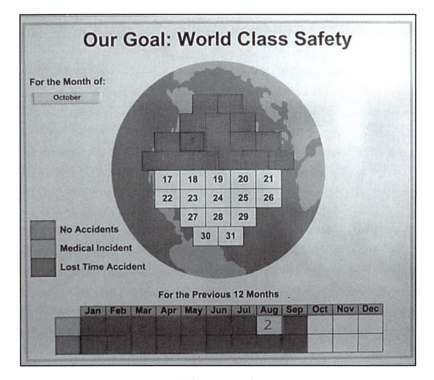

Figure #5
Typical Safety Measurement Board

Once the Leadership Team has established clear goals, it must IDENTIFY all opportunities to achieve the goals. Brainstorming is the tool that is used to generate ideas for potential projects. This, Step 3 in the process, is where a thorough understanding of the *Lean Concepts* is important. The team involved in Step 3 must have a rigorous understanding of the types of waste that are in the organization and take a total systems approach to

10 Steps to Successful Policy Deployment

1. Establish a Mission and Guiding Principles
2. Develop Business Goals
3. Brainstorm for Opportunities to Achieve Goals
4. Define Parameters to Value Opportunities
5. Establish Weighting Requirements, Rate Opportunities, and Prioritize
6. Conduct a Reality Check
7. Develop Lean Implementation Plan
8. Develop Bowling Chart
9. Countermeasures
10. Conducting Business Reviews

the products and/or services offered. The Leadership Team must have a clear view of customers, markets, products, and services.

This is an important step in the process and is crucial to the success of an organization. If the Step 3 team fails to identify the most important and significant opportunities for the organization, it may lead the organization down an incorrect path—a path which may not reach the goals stated in Step 2. We should not and must not work on the Leadership Team's "pet" projects—projects that would further individual power or turf expansion. The Policy Deployment process does contain a check step, Step 6. This "reality check" step requires that the team assure itself that if all the selected ideas from the brainstorming process were implemented, the goals, established in Step 2, would be met.

The Step 3 team must use out-of-the-box thinking, and the more ideas it can generate, the better. The team must not limit its thinking or imagination in how to improve the organization and in achieving the stated goals and objectives. When brainstorming opportunities, the Step 3 team should state the opportunities using the same format as for the organization's goals:

- Reduce scrap and rework from 6.3% of sales to less than 3% by the end of the fiscal year

- Reduce the time it takes to provide care for an emergency patient from 30 minutes to less than 5 minutes by the end of the year

- Reduce the time to process an order from 3 days to 30 minutes in the next 12 months

- Improve "hit rate" on request for quotes from 20% to 50% in the next 12 months

Next, begin to SCOPE the projects as a part of Step 3. Do this by paring ideas or establishing projects that can be completed in 60 to 90 days. How do you eat an elephant? You eat an elephant one bite at a time. Scope projects to get early wins and gain momentum—nothing breeds success like success. With every project that is completed the entire organization must celebrate its successes and failures. The organization sees each project as another step toward achieving its business goals and objectives.

When projects are not scoped so they can be completed in a reasonable time frame, people become discouraged and stop going to meetings. People do not see progress toward the organization's goals and lose motivation.

Scope projects that can be completed in a 90 day time frame so that a Lean Leader can spend the first 30 days preparing for a Kaizen Event. A Kaizen Event is a team of 5 to 12 people, dedicated full-time over a 3 to 5 day time period, and focused on accomplishing a specific activity in support of the goals set in Step 2. After the Kaizen Event, the team has 60 days to complete any open Action Items.

It should be noted here that no Kaizen team should ever be formed or empowered without a goal that ties into the organization's goals. Further explanation of Kaizen and Kaizen Events begins on page 46.

To ensure the organization is working on the correct projects, we must VALUE and PRIORITIZE these projects. This is accomplished in Steps 4 and 5. To properly value projects, we must evaluate them with regard to benefit of achieving the business goals versus effort. We assess effort with regard to the amount of people required, capital required, and the project risk.

10 STEPS TO SUCCESSFUL POLICY DEPLOYMENT

1. Establish a Mission and Guiding Principles

2. Develop Business Goals

3. Brainstorm for Opportunities to Achieve Goals

4. Define Parameters to Value Opportunities

5. Establish Weighting Requirements, Rate Opportunities, and Prioritize

6. Conduct a Reality Check

7. Develop Lean Implementation Plan

8. Develop Bowling Chart

9. Countermeasures

10. Conducting Business Reviews

√ Lean Overview

Once a prioritized list is made of all the opportunities required to achieve the business goals and objectives, we can muster up the most powerful resource an organization has—its people. World Class Enterprises empower teams to systematically attack each of these opportunities. Establish a team, the team's goal(s), scope, and guidelines for each opportunity. Commit resources by putting together cross-functional teams of people, train the teams, and launch the teams by empowering them to complete their task within the stated time frame.

One of the biggest mistakes an organization can make is to implement improvement initiatives such as Lean and then start working projects that are not linked to the business goals or objectives. The Lean initiative will be perceived as something to do in addition to the already busy and hectic work schedule if it is not linked to the business goals.

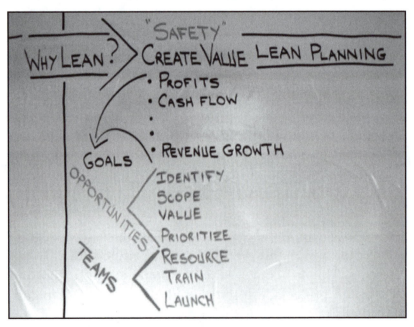

Figure #6
Lean Planning Component Elements

20

Lean Overview ✓

This list of opportunities to achieve the business goals and objectives, together with the associated teams (completed in Step 7), will begin to form the foundation of our Lean Planning process. The Lean Planning process also needs to incorporate the Lean Concepts, Lean Tools, and Lean Culture.

By establishing the business goals, the Leadership Team has begun to develop a vision and a sense of urgency for what the organization needs to look like in one, three, and five years down the road. By developing the prioritized list of opportunities that are linked to the business objectives of the organization, you have begun to develop a path to achieve the vision. By empowering teams, you have enabled the most powerful resource an organization has in achieving its vision—its people! Positive and rapid improvement is possible when everyone in the organization pulls in the same direction. In many organizations this positive and rapid improvement cannot occur because of organizational "brickwalls" disguised as members of the management team (usually supervisors or middle managers). Lack of middle management and supervisor "buy-in" to the Lean process is the third of 10 reasons why Lean implementations fail.

These initial steps fit nicely into the five change implementation prerequisites as defined by John P. Kotter in his book *Leading Change*. The change implementation prerequisites that must be implemented by the Leadership Team are:

1. Establishing a Sense of Urgency

    ♦ Individuals or organizations do not change without a sense of urgency to do so. The Leadership Team must create this sense of urgency by communicating a current or future threat to the organization.

2. <mark>Creating the Guiding Coalition</mark>

- Put together a group with enough power to lead and guide the organization through the change. This group should represent a cross section of the organization.

- Get the group to work together like a team.

3. <mark>Developing a Vision and Strategy</mark>

- A vision is a broad description of the future state of the organization. Create a vision to help direct the change effort.

- Develop strategies for achieving that vision.

4. <mark>Communicating the Change Vision</mark>

- Use every vehicle possible to constantly communicate the new vision and strategies.

- Have the guiding coalition role-model the behavior expected of employees.

5. <mark>Empowering all Associates</mark>

- Get rid of obstacles.

- Change systems or structures that undermine the change vision.

- Encourage risk taking and nontraditional ideas, activities, and actions.

Lean Overview

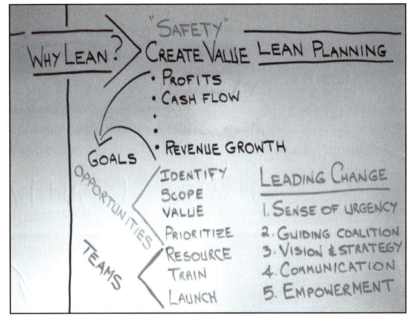

Figure #7
Leading Change Element of Lean Planning

Additional comments on the Lean Planning component will be covered after the other three components of Lean—Lean Concepts, Lean Tools, and Lean Culture—have been discussed.

Lean Concepts

The next component of our Lean System that we will discuss is Lean Concepts. In this component, we must understand that Lean is the elimination of waste so as to improve the FLOW of information and material. The concept of flow is critical since it, or the lack of it, determines the lead time for our products or services. Waste in our business processes impedes or stops flow. When we talk about improving flow, we take a system approach. A World Class Enterprise would look at the flow, or lack of flow, from the quotation of a job to the collection of cash—quote to cash. Or, in a not-for-profit

√ Lean Overview

organization, from the time the client requests a service to the time the money/funding is collected/received for the service.

Waste is defined as anything other than the *minimum* amount of people, time, equipment, material, parts, and space required to *add value* to the product, service, or information product.

Sitting in a doctor's office is not value-added time. The customer is not paying the doctor for the pleasure of sitting in the waiting room. The patient is willing to pay for quality time with the doctor to properly diagnose his/her illness and prescribe the best possible treatment.

The customer is not paying a manufacturing company to enter an order into a computer system or generate some financial report. Customers are paying for a product or service that conforms to their requirements. Customers are willing to pay you for a machining, welding, stamping, or assembly operation. They are most likely not willing to pay you to transport material around your plant or create and manage large amounts of inventory.

There are eight types of waste exhibited by most organizations, whether they be manufacturing or service oriented:

1. Scrap/rework/inspection/reconciliation

2. Transportation

3. Associate motion

4. Associate wait time

5. Inventory (raw, WIP, finished goods)

6. Overproduction

7. Overprocessing

8. Underutilization of Human Resources

A key characteristic of a good leader and a distinguishing feature of a World Class Enterprise is that they hate waste and have a passion to improve the flow of information and material throughout the entire system. They empower their people and create an environment where it is okay to wage a "war on waste."

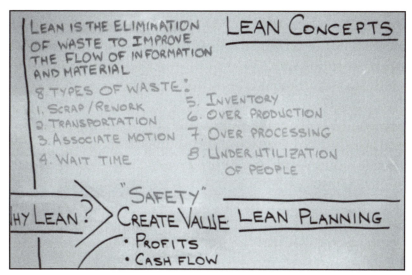

Figure #8
Lean Concepts Component

Lean defines a clear path from the receipt of the order to the customer's receiving dock, and ensures every activity along that path is focused on adding value (waste-free) as defined by the customer.

Adding value generally means that you are doing something the customer cares about, which means the customer is willing to pay for this activity. It also means that you are changing the "shape" or "form" of the part or information packet and it means you are performing this activity correctly, the first time.

Lean Tools

With the creation of organizational goals using the Lean Planning component, and the understanding of how wasteful activities in our organizations prevent the achievement of those goals (Lean Concepts), the discussion can now turn to understanding the tools of Lean. The Lean toolbox (see Figure #9) can identify what waste is preventing the organization from reaching its goals and also provides the tools to eliminate/reduce the identified waste.

THE POWER OF LEAN SIGMA PROBLEM SOLVING

Lean's goal is to eliminate waste.

Six Sigma's goal is to eliminate process variation.

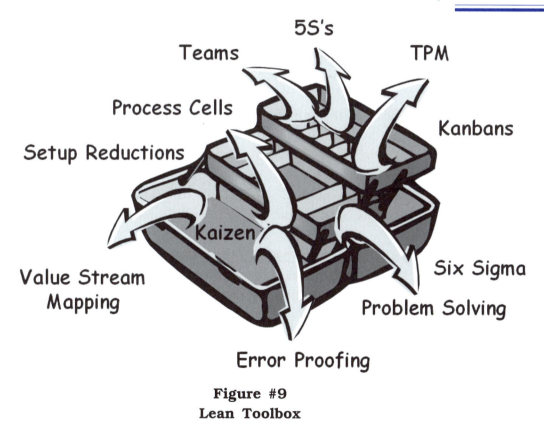

**Figure #9
Lean Toolbox**

The Lean toolbox is the area where most organizations get confused. They think that by implementing some of the Lean tools they will have a Lean organization (they skip Lean Planning and Lean Culture).

Lean Overview

The following are some of the key Lean tools with a brief description of each tool. For a more comprehensive description of each tool referenced, see *Implementing World Class Manufacturing, Business Manual, 2nd Edition* by Larry Rubrich & Mattie Watson.

5S

The 5S's are about creating a safe, clean, and organized business. They attack organizational waste related to:

- Lost time/injury accidents
- Searching, hunting, or looking for anything including office or computer files

Since having a safe, clean, and organized business is the foundation of becoming a World Class Enterprise, 5S is usually the first tool deployed by most organizations. The other advantage to implementing 5S first is that with the discipline of 5S in place, the rest of the Lean tools are easier to implement.

Sort, Straighten/Set in Order, Sweep/Shine, Schedule/Standardize, and Sustain represent the five elements of implementing 5S. We need to be able to Sort what is needed from that which is not needed. One general rule is if it has not been used in the last 30 days and will not be used in the next 30 days, then you need to move it out of the area. Straighten/Set in Order means to establish a place for everything and put everything in its place. Another general rule is that anyone should be able to find something in your area in 30 seconds or less. Sweep/Shine the area completely using a top down approach. Clean and paint as required to make things look like new. Design ways to contain messes to keep future cleanup small. Establish a plan or Schedule/

"World Class facilities develop beginning with the 5S's, and facilities that fail, fall apart beginning with the 5S's."

HIROYUKI HIRANO
5 PILLARS OF THE VISUAL WORKPLACE

Standardize a method to keep the area clean, neat, and organized. The last step is the most difficult and that is to Sustain the gains of the first four steps. In this step an audit process is established that would not only ensure that the gains are held but also make recommendations on how to continuously improve the area.

This tool applies in all businesses and in every area. Again, 5S is the foundation for all the other tools. If you cannot maintain a safe, clean, and organized work environment, you can never be a World Class Enterprise.

Value Stream Mapping (VSM)

Value Stream Mapping (VSM) is the only Lean tool that will not eliminate waste—its sole purpose is to help organizations identify the waste that is preventing them from reaching their organizational goals. Once the waste is identified, the appropriate waste elimination Lean tool can be pulled from the toolbox and deployed to eliminate the waste.

Value Streaming Mapping creates a one page picture (although it may be a very large page—see Figure #10) of a process, identifying all the steps, sequence, touches, and times. Many organizations start by mapping the "system cycle time"—from the time a customer requests a product or service to the time the customer receives a completed product or service. VSM is most effective at identifying how to improve system efficiency.

√ *Lean Overview*

**Figure #10
Value Stream Mapping**

It should be noted that VSM is the most misused of all the Lean tools. Often maps are created with no specific organizational goal or improvement in mind other than to map a process. Since most organizations have hundreds of problems which can be revealed by the map—where do you start? It is recommended that the following four-step VSM process be used:

1) Pick the product, product family, service, production, or administrative process to map (improve). An improvement goal(s) is required. Again, this goal should tie into the organizational goals.

2) Create the "Current State" VSM (CSVSM).

3) Create the "Future State" VSM (FSVSM). This map must meet the goal(s) established in #1 above.

4) Develop an action plan (Kaizen newspaper) to make the FSVSM the new CSVSM.

By creating Value Stream Maps, an organization begins to "see" the waste in the organization and can systematically attack the waste.

There are two key metrics that we calculate when conducting a Value Stream Mapping activity. The first one is TAKT time.

$$\text{TAKT Time} = \frac{\text{Total Available Time}}{\text{Customer Demand}}$$
(For the Same Time Increment)

TAKT is a German word that means "Time Beat" or "Rhythm." Takt Time represents the heartbeat of your organization. This is the pace your organization needs to work to in order to meet customer demand.

The other key metric when doing a Value Stream Map is System Cycle Time. We refer to System Cycle Time as the actual physical time it takes to process an order in days including weekends—this is what the customer sees. We include days of raw, WIP, and finished goods inventory (because we can artificially reduce the time it takes to process a customer's order by creating large amounts of inventory), and it includes the time it takes to collect the money for the products or services.

In Value Stream Mapping we calculate "percent of value added time."

$$\text{Percent Value Added Time} = \frac{\text{Total Value Added Time}}{\text{Total Processing Time}} \times 100$$
(including days of inventory)

Do not be surprised if the "Percent Value Added Analysis" is below 2%.

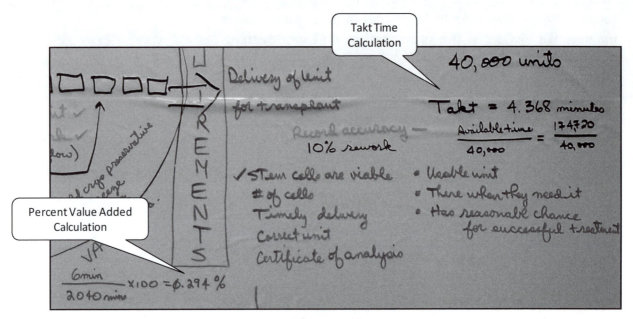

Figure #11
Value Added and TAKT Time Analysis

Total Productive Maintenance (TPM)

Total Productive Maintenance is a method for continuously improving the effectiveness of all processes and equipment through the involvement of all the people in an organization (not just the maintenance department). This involvement in TPM activities includes the equipment operator, supervision, management, purchasing, engineering, and maintenance.

TPM improves quality, productivity, lead time, and delivery by focusing on improving equipment uptime and the effectiveness of that uptime.

Overall Equipment Effectiveness (OEE) is the key metric of TPM and there are three elements of OEE: uptime of the machine, the efficiency at which the machine is running, and the quality of the product coming off the machine.

TPM is an important prerequisite to high performance manufacturing Process Cells.

Process Cells

A process cell is a grouping of desks or machines dedicated to the production of a particular information or physical product or to a family of products. Cells bring together a small team of people who are capable of completing a job or task from start to finish. Cells are formed by grouping together all the people who "touch" a particular information or physical product, for example, order entry cells (Figures #12 and #13).

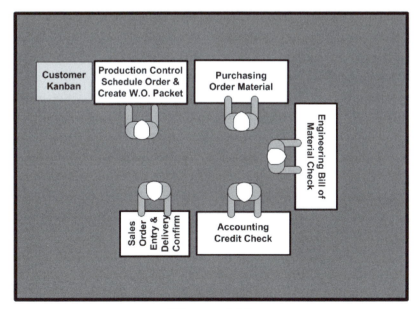

Figure #12
Administrative Cell Proposed Layout

√ *Lean Overview*

**Figure #13
Administrative Cell**

It could just as easily be a loan application cell or mortgage approval cell. The desks or machines are usually in a "U" shape formation and the physical material or information packet is passed or moved in a counterclockwise fashion.

Process cells eliminate business waste by:

♦ Reducing or eliminating work-in-process inventory thereby shortening the process lead time (and the System Cycle Time)

♦ Improving product quality

♦ Reducing motion and transportation

While improving:

- Communication
- Teamwork (everyone in the cell has a common goal)
- Productivity
- Ability to cross-train associates

The team will become autonomous (if that is the part of the organization's desired culture) and thereby can make decisions concerning their work process as long as they are continuously making improvements regarding how the team is supporting the organization's goals.

Change-Over or Set-Up Reduction

Like a pit crew for a race car, a Change-Over team will continuously reduce the time from when a machine stops running the last good part "A" to the time it starts running a good part "B". This concept applies to production machines in a manufacturing company, the Turn-Around Time of an operating room in a hospital, and "shut downs" in a construction company.

Change-Over reduction eliminates business waste by:

- Reducing or eliminating the need for work-in-process inventory thereby shortening the process lead time (and the System Cycle Time)

While improving:

- Product quality

♦ Organizational capacity

♦ Organizational flexibility in responding to changing customer needs

♦ On-time deliveries

5S activities—"A place for everything and everything in its place"—play a key role in Change-Over Time reductions.

Inventory Kanbans

Single piece continuous flow is the most effective and cost-efficient way to produce or process anything. However, we also realize that this is not always possible. There are steps within the process that run at dissimilar speeds. If the process steps or equipment speeds cannot be synchronized or changed, we need to inject a buffer inventory into the systems so as to simulate single piece continuous flow.

Kanbans are signals which automate the replenishment of materials and supplies from internal or external suppliers to the buffer inventories. Kanbans reduce outages and shortages of materials and supplies which improves customer service levels. Kanbans support "pull production" and continuous flow, since material is not produced at the supplier until a signal to replenish material is received from the customer. Using this approach, Kanbans will reduce overall inventory levels (a 30% reduction on average).

In a Lean world, we want a system that has one piece continuous flow. When we cannot have single piece continuous flow, work is pulled through the processes rather than push work through the processes. Work is pulled from a Kanban, whether it is material from a manufacturing Kanban or patient files from an office Kanban. The concept works everywhere.

Kanbans eliminate business waste by:

- Reducing raw material, work-in-process, and finished goods inventory

- Eliminating overproduction

- Reducing paperwork

- Reducing materials and supplies shortages and outages

While improving:

- Product flow

- Product lead times

- Cash flow

Lean Sigma Problem Solving

This is where Lean and Six Sigma come together. Simply stated, Lean is about the elimination of waste and Six Sigma is about the reduction or elimination of process variation. Ultimately, most organizations need to implement both Lean and Six Sigma on their journey to become a World Class Enterprise.

Lean eliminates waste to improve the flow of information and material. Lean improves process speed—velocity. The key metric in Lean is Total System Efficiency from quote to cash.

THE POWER OF LEAN SIGMA PROBLEM SOLVING

Lean's goal is to eliminate waste.

Six Sigma's goal is to eliminate process variation.

ULTIMATE LEAN SIGMA GOAL

Waste free processes operating at Six Sigma capability

Six Sigma uses process control and capability to eliminate variation. Its key metric is defects per million opportunities. In a Six Sigma world, a process would only have 3.4 defects per million opportunities. The structured problem solving methodology, used to eliminate process variation in Six Sigma, is known as DMAIC (Define, Measure, Analyze, Improve, and Control).

Regardless of which structured problem solving methodology you use, the purpose is to eliminate systemic process problems. It is very difficult to get into single piece continuous flow when defects are being produced in the process.

Error Proofing/Mistake Proofing— Prevention versus Inspection

Many American managers believe that we cannot do things "right the first time." They have been conditioned to believe that the concept of "zero defects" is impossible. Consequently, a lot of money is spent inspecting and reworking or redoing things to get them right. In fact, there are companies that believe so strongly that "zero defects" is impossible that they want their customers to inspect the product for them. Figure #14 is such an example.

Stop the practice of putting in inspection stations and institutionalizing fancy fixes that communicate to the organization that it is okay not to do things right. Create an organization that is willing to systematically attack all processes. Organizations have process problems, not people problem. Stop the practice of attacking people; implement a practice of preventing systemic process problems.

Figure #14
Inspection Versus Prevention

Occasionally people and machines do make errors or mistakes. The goal of Error Proofing/Mistake Proofing is to prevent these mistakes from turning into information or physical product defects that may reach the customer.

The ultimate goal of Error Proofing is to produce perfect information or physical product quality. While often thought to be a prohibitively expensive way to produce a product, perfect product quality is actually the least expensive way to produce. Perfect product quality requires us to "Do It Right The First Time" (DIRTFT) for every step in the process. When the waste of scrap, rework, remake, and reassembly are eliminated, costs are reduced.

Error Proofing is most effective when it is implemented as part of the information or physical product design process. There are four types of Error Proofing (in decreasing order of effectiveness):

- Prevention—designed so it cannot be done wrong

- Prevention in station—the computer, tooling, or fixturing prevents the operator from doing it wrong

- Detection in station—if the operator does it wrong, he or she is made aware of it so immediate correction can occur

- Detection at downstream station—the operator's internal customer is able to detect the defect

Using Error Proofing in most companies requires a fairly large change in the culture. Today, organizational cultures tend to consciously support the "brooming under the rug" or hiding of problems. Associates that raise these issues are often admonished as complainers or whiners. The messenger is shot!

However, in a World Class Enterprise, associates are rewarded when they raise their hand and admit that an error has occurred. This is seen as an opportunity to improve. In Toyota, having no problems is a problem. Once a mistake occurs and is identified, a small team gathers and develops a simple, elegant, and inexpensive way to prevent the error from ever recurring. Lean focuses on low cost or no cost solutions.

Spaghetti Diagrams

We already know that people motion and the transportation of hard copy information or materials are considered waste. Often used in combination with other Lean tools like 5S, Process Cells, VSM, or Setup Reduction, a Spaghetti Diagram is a useful tool for reviewing the distance and path that people, objects, materials, and information packets must follow in a process.

Using this tool requires tracing out the material or information flow as it travels step-by-step through the process, often traveling from department to department (see Figure #15).

With Error Proofing, Zero Defects is Possible!

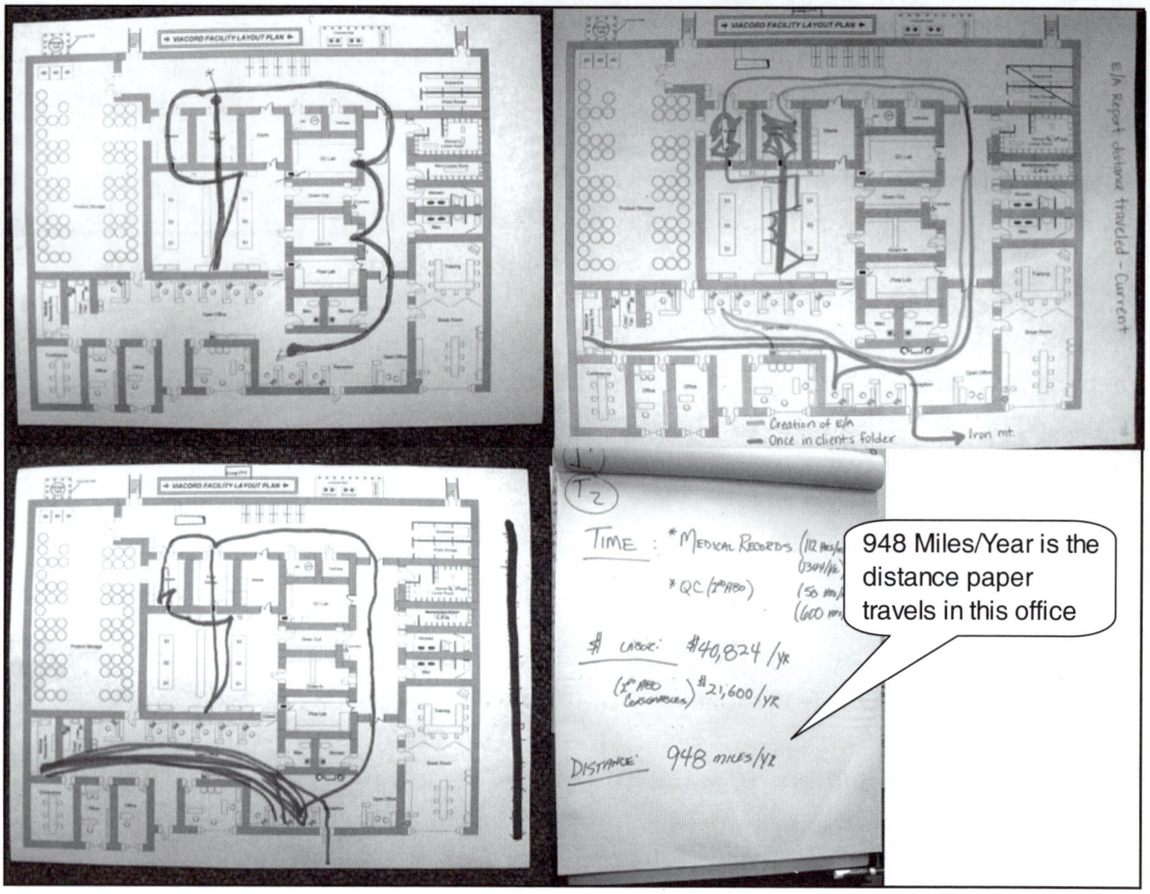

√ *Lean Overview*

Figure #15
Spaghetti Diagrams

948 Miles/Year is the distance paper travels in this office

Actual measurements are made using a scalable office/plant layout, through the use of a measuring wheel (in feet), or pedometer (in steps). Once this analysis is conducted, the team can brainstorm opportunities to reduce or eliminate non-value added activities. Often this means moving the people or departments who touch the information or materials closer together. The elimination of this waste improves the System Cycle Time.

Visual Management

One of the distinguishing features of World Class Enterprises is teamwork. For teamwork to occur in any organization, the following four elements must be in place:

1) High levels of two-way communication

2) Team members with diverse backgrounds

3) Common purpose/motivated by mission

4) Common goals/measurements

The goal of communication in a teamwork environment is to make sure everyone knows what's going on so they all pull in the same direction. Great two-way communication occurs in two parts, verbal and visual.

Visual Management includes Visual Standard Work which is the documented method for operators and equipment to work together to produce a quality product or provide a quality service while minimizing all forms of waste. It documents the safest, best and easiest way to do a job and is focused on the process or procedure (not the person or the outcome).

You know you have good Visual Management when a casual visitor can come into your facility and understand the information flow, material flow, and how the organization is performing without having to ask questions. See Figures #16 and #17.

√ *Lean Overview*

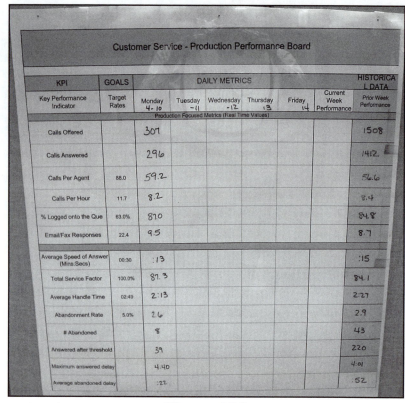

**Figure #16
Administrative Production Board**

44

Lean Overview √

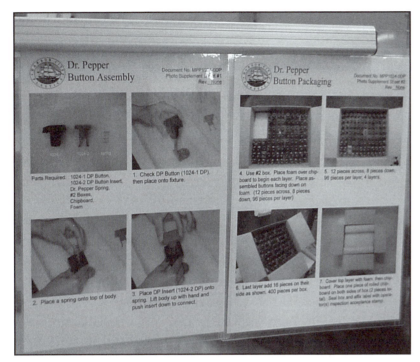

**Figure #17
Assembly Standard Work**

Visual Management is a key tool in measuring how the company is responding to the deployment of the organization's goals in Steps 7 and 8.

√ Lean Overview

No Kaizen Team should ever be formed or empowered without a goal that ties into the organizations goals

[handwritten note: goals must tie to organizations goals.]

Kaizen

Kaizen is a Japanese word that means to "change for the good"—doing little things better every day—continuous improvement. The target of Kaizen is cost reduction through the elimination of waste at all levels of the process. Kaizen has become part of the Japanese culture in manufacturing, especially at organizations like Toyota.

Unfortunately, Americans have trouble thinking in terms of slow and continuous improvement. Americans want giant steps, dramatic improvement, and home runs, so there is a difference between how the Japanese and Americans use Kaizen. For U.S. Companies, a Kaizen Event is a team of people (5-12) who will spend approximately three to five days focused on an organizational process or cell to accomplish a particular goal. The intent is to cause rapid, dramatic performance improvements in the process. Thirty days prior to the event, the Lean Facilitator collects data and prepares for the event. A Kaizen Event starts with the Lean Facilitator training the team on one of the Lean Tools to ensure common understanding and concludes once the team has accomplished the initial goal. Near the end of the Kaizen Event the team elects a team leader. The team leader and the team then have 60 days from the end of the event to complete all open action items on the Kaizen Newspaper.

Kaizen Events are a powerful improvement tool! Like VSM, Kaizen Events unfortunately are often misused. They have become an "end all" to themselves. Organizations do Kaizen Events just to do them. These events are often called spot, point, or drive-by Kaizen Events. Again, when examined, organizations are found to have hundreds of wasteful activities that cannot all be elimi-

46

nated at once. Use Kaizen Events to focus only on the improvements which support the organization's goals that were deployed throughout the company.

Kaizen Events should ultimately be scheduled using this "pull" strategy. Early on in the Lean implementation, it may be necessary for the company's Lean Facilitator to "push" or tell a particular area to do a Kaizen Event. This may be based on a particular team operating below their committed to goal (which supports the achievement of the organization's goals). Once all the teams and areas of an organization "own" their goals and measurements, they will pull Kaizen Event help from the Lean Facilitator when they find themselves off target.

Lean Tools Summary

All of these tools are powerful. When they are used correctly they can cause a lot of good things to happen. When they are misused or abused, they can cause bad things to happen. Without the connection between the use of the Lean Tools and the business objectives of the organization, people do not understand "WHY" they are doing what they are doing.

Figure #18 shows how the Lean Tools are connected to the business goals and objectives of an organization or vice versa. Let's say an organization has a goal to improve profitability. This same organization identifies, during the planning process, that they have a significant amount of scrap in their organization. Let us also say that this organization has a substantial number of customer complaints, returns, and warranty issues. By using the Problem Solving tool to reduce defects, rather than using inspection to detect defects, we will reduce costs and improve profitability. At the same time, using

> **Without the connection between the use of the Lean Tools and the business objectives of the organization, people do not understand "WHY" they are doing what they are doing.**

√ Lean Overview

> Problem Solving to prevent defects from reaching your customer will result in greater customer satisfaction, reaping more repeat business, and resulting in an increase in revenue.
>
> In the same vein, an organization may have a goal to service more people with the same available resources. Let's look at providing medical care for a patient. We may decide to use the Value Stream Mapping tool to look at all activities from the time the patient requests service to the time treatment and payment is received. A team can then use this tool to drive out all the wasted activities to achieve the given goal.

Lean's Impact on Business Goals / Objectives				
		Impact On		
		Profitability	Cash Flow	Revenue Growth
Lean Tools	5S	X	X	O
	Process Cells	X	X	O
	TPM	X	X	O
	Change-Over Reduction	X	X	O
	Problem Solving	X	X	X
	Error Proofing	X	X	X
	Inventory Kanbans	O	X	O
	VSM	O	X	X
	Kaizen	X	X	X
	Visual Management	X	X	O
	Spaghetti Diagrams	X	X	O
X = Large Impact				
O = Lesser Impact				

Figure #18

48

These tools would be used by a team of people in a Kaizen event. When we conduct Kaizen Events, the team is encouraged to wear something distinctive like a vest, hat, or T-shirt (see Figure #19). The reason for this is to give the Kaizen Event visibility to the entire organization and to communicate the significance of the team's activity. Everyone should know that this team is working on the most important improvement initiative in the organization at this time. Everyone knows that there is a direct correlation between this Kaizen Event and the Business Objectives of the organization. Everyone knows that once this team completes its goal the organization will have taken one more important step toward the vision the Leadership Team has established.

Figure #19

A summary of the Lean tools we have discussed is shown in Figure #20.

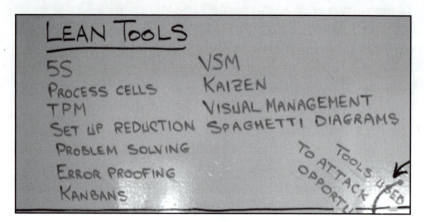

Figure #20

Appendix A describes two additional Lean tools that are called "Advanced" Lean tools—Production Preparation Planning (3P) and Design for Manufacturability and Assembly (DFMA). Generally, these are not introduced until the organization has a firm foundation with the basic tools (year 3-5 of the Lean implementation) and everyone is pulling in the same direction through the use of Policy Deployment.

Lean Culture

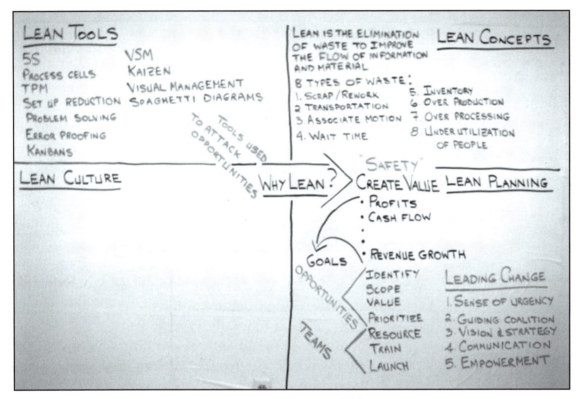

Figure #21

The fourth component of understanding how to implement Lean is establishing a Lean Culture (See Figure #21). This is the component that makes it all happen, the component that musters the organization's most important resource, its people, to create a "war on waste."

The only major competitive weapon an organization has is its people. Most organizations do not have a lot of patents or technology that can protect them from their competitors or create barriers to entry into their markets. Generally speaking, it is an organization's people that make the difference.

√ *Lean Overview*

Volumes of books have been written on the importance of creating a positive, people-based culture within an organization. It would appear that most of the leadership in organizations know and agree that people can make a difference. Then why does it seem so difficult to create a positive, people-based culture? Why does management insist on making all the decisions without the involvement of the people working in the processes?

To understand culture better, let us explore several questions about culture. What is culture? How do we acquire culture? What purpose does culture serve? Why would any culture change? How does this apply to Corporate Cultures?

What is culture? William A. Haviland in his textbook, *Cultural Anthropology* defines it as:

> *"Culture: A set of rules and standards shared by members of a society, which when acted upon the members, produce behavior that falls within a range the members consider proper and acceptable."*

How do we acquire culture? Culture is a learned process. We begin to learn our culture from our mother and father, aunts and uncles, brothers and sisters, and our extended family. We learn what is right and what is wrong. We learn what behavior is acceptable and what behavior is unacceptable. Eventually this is extended into the community. We continue to learn our culture from friends, teachers, a religious cleric, maybe from a law enforcement agent. We continue to learn our culture which is reflected in our behavior.

Culture is a learned process. We begin to learn our culture from our mother and father, aunts and uncles, brothers and sisters, and our extended family. We learn what is right and what is wrong. We learn what behavior is acceptable and what behavior is unacceptable.

"All culture is learned rather than biologically inherited. One learns one's culture by growing up with it. Ralph Linton referred to culture as humanity's "social heredity." The process whereby culture is transmitted from one generation to the next is called enculturation. Through enculturation one learns the socially appropriate way of satisfying one's biological determined needs. It is important to distinguish between the needs themselves, which are not learned, and the learned ways in which they are satisfied. The biological needs of humans are the same as those of other animals: food, shelter, companionship, self-defense, and sexual gratification. Each culture determines in its own way how these needs will be met."

What purpose does culture serve? If culture guides our behavior and allows us to meet our biological needs, then culture helps us SURVIVE in the environment in which we live and work. Survival is a very strong word. Without culture, everyone in a society would act or behave differently. No one would be able to anticipate someone else's behavior, and no one would understand why people behave the way they do. Life would be very chaotic. Biological needs would not be met and eventually the society would either adapt or die!

"A culture cannot survive if it does not satisfy certain basic needs of its members. The extent to which a culture achieves the fulfillment of these needs will determine its ultimate success. 'Success' is measured by the values of the culture itself rather than by those of an outsider. A culture must provide for the production and distribution of goods

If culture guides our behavior and allows us to meet our biological needs, then culture helps us SURVIVE in the environment in which we live and work.

and services considered necessary for life. It must provide for biological continuity through the reproduction of its members. It must acculturate new members so that they can become functioning adults. It must maintain order among it members. It must likewise maintain order between members and outsiders. Finally, it must motivate its members to survive and engage in those activities necessary for survival."

Why would any culture change? Culture is a learned process that aids us in meeting our biological needs, and helps us survive in the environment in which we live and work. If the environment changes, then the culture would have to change in order to increase the chances for its members to survive. Notice we say "increase" our chances of surviving. There are no guarantees in life. The more flexible and adaptable a culture is to an ever-changing environment, the more chance it has in adapting or responding to environmental pressures.

> **There are no guarantees in life. The more flexible and adaptable a culture is to an ever-changing environment, the more chance it has in adapting or responding to environmental pressures.**

"All cultures change over a period of time, although not always as rapidly or as massively as many are doing today. Changes take place in response to such events as environmental crises, intrusion of outsiders, or modification of behavior and values within the culture."

How does this apply to corporate cultures? Organizations are no different than any social group. They have their own language and people learn the culture of the organization from the very first day they start their jobs—sometimes even sooner. They learn what behavior is acceptable and what behavior is unacceptable.

They learn the organization's culture from their supervisor (parent), they learn it from other associates in their department (siblings), and they learn it from other associates in the organization (extended family).

People learn their "place" in the organization, they learn their role and responsibility. They learn what behavior management expects from them. We credit Fredrick Winslow Taylor for our current scientific management style. Taken from *Factory Physics*, 2nd Edition:

> *"It is easy in hindsight to give credit to many individuals for seeking to rationalize the practice of management. But until Frederick W. Taylor (1856–1915), no one generated the sustained interest, active following, and systematic framework necessary to plausibly proclaim management as a discipline. It was Taylor who persistently and vocally called for the use of science in management. It was Taylor who presented his ideas as a coherent system in both his publications and his many oral presentations. It was Taylor who, with the help of his associates, implemented his system in many plants. And it was Taylor who lies buried under the epithet 'father of scientific management'.*

> *"But what were Taylor's ideas that accord him such a lofty position in the history of management? On the surface, Taylor was an almost fanatic champion of efficiency ... the core of his management system consisted of breaking down the production process into its component parts and improving the efficiency of each. In essence, Taylor was trying to do for work units what Whitney had done*

for material units: standardize them and make them interchangeable. Work standards, which he applied to activities ranging from shoveling coal to precision machining, represented the work rate that should be attainable by a "first-class man."

We should not be critical of the contribution that Fredrick W. Taylor made to American management style. Back in the early 1900s, given the environment, it was very effective. It worked. It allowed a lot of immigrants coming into the United States, fleeing Europe before World War I, to get jobs. People did not necessarily speak English. American management (starting with Henry Ford) broke work down into component parts and instructed people how to do their jobs. Management did not want workers to think; they could not understand most of what was said anyway. Management just wanted them to do their jobs. Management did not want their minds, just their bodies.

So why would any organization want to change their culture? It comes back to survival and the environment. If the environment changes, then the culture has to change in order to improve the organization's chances of survival. The environment is changing. We are now competing in a global marketplace. To successfully compete in a global economy, an organization must take full advantage of all the resources in the organization.

Taken from Free Management Library: A Complete Integrated On-line Library For Nonprofits & For-Profits:

"The concept of culture is particularly important when attempting to manage organization-wide change. Practitioners are coming to realize that, despite the best-laid

plans, organizational change must include not only changing structures and processes, but also changing the corporate culture as well.

"There has been a great deal of literature generated over the past decade about the concept of organizational culture—particularly in regard to learning how to change organizational culture. Organizational change efforts are rumored to fail the vast majority of the time. Usually, this failure is credited to lack of understanding about the strong role of culture and the role it plays in organizations. That is one of the reasons that many strategic planners now place as much emphasis on identifying strategic values as they do mission and vision."

We define or translate "strategic values" into behavioral expectations. It is difficult to observe "values" strategic or otherwise. However, we can observe behavior that reflects our values, or identify behavior that goes against our values. For example, if an organization decides that they want a Lean Culture, one of the values or behavior expectations they must state is that everyone will maintain a safe, clean, and organized workplace. It then becomes clear. There is no doubt what the Leadership Team expects to see. Everyone will need to use 5S to achieve this behavioral expectation.

When asked, most organizations will tell you that their culture has changed over the last five to ten years and that their culture will most likely change again over the next five to ten years. If that is the case, why would any organization leave this culture change to chance? Why would you not determine the culture you want in your organization and put a plan into place to make it happen? We have already established that culture is a learned process. People learn their culture through language. Lean creates a common language and a common culture in your organization. It provides an environment for people with different backgrounds, experiences, educational levels, and skills to work together for a common good.

There are four elements that can be used to impact culture or affect culture change in an organization: leadership, communication, empowerment, and teamwork (See Figure #22).

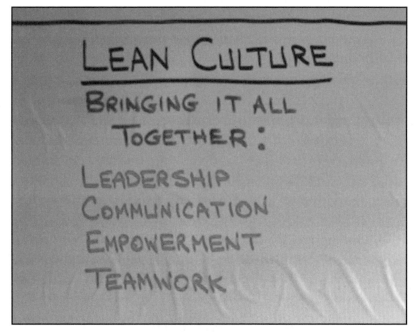

Figure #22

Leadership

All organizations have a culture (positive or negative) that is developed, formed, and modified over years based on the actions, examples, and behavioral model presented by the Leadership Team to the rest of the organization.

Unfortunately, the responsibility and accountability for the development of a positive organizational culture must be missing from CEO, COO, president, and plant manager job descriptions since culture development is most often set adrift to develop on its own at the supervisory level. Because many supervisors, brought up through the organization, were trained (and still are) in a "Taylor like" mindset, a negative culture is developed. When the organization is not performing well, the Leadership Team then blames all the people who they say have "bad attitudes" and "don't care about the company."

> We were recently asked to attend a Leadership Team meeting at a company that was having difficulty sustaining the implementation of Lean within their organization. While we sat around the conference table discussing the symptoms, a floor supervisor, who had only been with the company four to five months, spoke up. "The problem with this company is the people—they all have bad attitudes and they don't care." In pursuing this discussion, we asked the Director of HR if they were hiring people with "bad attitudes." The HR Director assured the team that the HR screening processes brought in good people, a point no one on the team disagreed with. We then asked the Leadership Team to consider how good employees, who after a few years of exposure to the environment (culture) that the Leadership Team had created in the organization, turned into employees with bad attitudes who didn't care about the company. Embarrassed by recognizing the truth in these discussions, the Leadership Team quickly refocused their efforts to how they could create an environment where good people could excel.

√ Lean Overview

Upon a "root cause" examination of this good employee to bad attitude employee transformation, cultural elements that would prevent a successful Lean implementation are found:

- People are told to use their arms and legs to do their job—not their brains

- They are not asked for their ideas—only told what to do

- They are not trained in anything other than by OJT

- They are not asked to participate in securing the company's (and their) future

- While they are told they are on the "team," no one communicates with them other than to place blame

> **THE TOP 3 REASONS LEAN IMPLEMENTATIONS FAIL:**
>
> 1) Lack of Top Management Leadership and Support
>
> 2) Lack of Communication
>
> 3) Lack of Middle Management/ Supervisor Buy-In

The Leadership Team can jump-start the culture change process by issuing organizational behavioral expectations (more on this in Step 1). Behavioral expectations or codes of conduct are short statements, usually in the form of a laminated pocket card, that are "a set of rules or standards" that members of the organization use to guide their behavior and actions.

It should be noted that the behavioral expectations will only produce culture change if they are modeled by the Leadership Team. Since the culture change process can take years, the Leadership Team must be committed to the guidelines as a new way of doing business.

60

The Wiremold Company, an example of a very successful Lean implementation in an American company, used a Code of Conduct statement to reset the Wiremold culture at the start of their Lean journey. (These figures are from Dick Ryan's "The Wiremold Story." Dick was the VP of Sales & Marketing at Wiremold).

The status of the Wiremold organization at the start of the journey is presented in the following chart:

Wiremold's Status in 1990-1991

- Low Profits
- No Cash
- No Growth
- Bad Customer Service
- Losing Market Share

Time for a New Approach

Early on in its journey, Wiremold developed the following premise that set the foundation for its culture change and its Lean implementation:

Fundamental Wiremold Premise

Companies are just collections (teams) of people trying to outperform other collections of people to satisfy a set of customers

The best, most motivated and focused team wins

The Wiremold Code of Conduct then established the behaviors to build their team:

CODE OF CONDUCT

- Respect Others
- Tell The Truth
- Be Fair
- Try New Ideas
- Ask Why
- Keep Your Promises
- Do Your Share

To reinforce the code at Wiremold, the Leadership Team members would circulate amongst the workforce on a regular basis, asking team members to "tell me one part of the code."

With the Code of Conduct in place, Wiremold implemented the following Lean Tools throughout the organization:

- 5c's (5S)
- Visual Management
- One piece flow lines
- Setup Reduction
- Kanbans

At the same time they set up measurements that would help them achieve their organizational goals that were set in their Lean Planning sessions:

- Customer Service
- Productivity
- Inventory/working capital turns
- Reduction in defects (quality)
- 5c's and degree of visual management
- Profit sharing

By 1999, Wiremold had achieved the following results:

Wiremold in the 90's

1990 - 1999

Sales	↑ 4.1x
Operating Profit	↑ 13.9x

Just Scratching the Surface

In 2000, the Wiremold organization was sought out and purchased by a company for $505.07 per share. This share value represented a 1,861% increase from 1990.

Wiremold did many things right and achieved outstanding results while, in their own words, "just scratching the surface." Their story provides an outline that would serve most companies well. This *Policy Deployment & Lean Implementation Planning* book follows the same outline.

Generally organizations in the United States take their most technically competent people and promote them to be supervisors or managers. This does not make them good supervisors or managers or leaders. The same tools these people used to become technically competent are not the same tools that they will need to be good leaders. As we have already stated: one of the most important characteristic of a good leader is to provide a vision for where the organization is going to be one, three, and five years down the road and a map on how to get there. Additionally, good leaders must be able to communicate and motivate the organization to implement the vision.

While working for the University of Portland a number of years ago, the author was trained in a Leadership series that was provided by Vital Learning. After the initial indoctrination, we started to train numerous managers in various industries throughout the Portland area. This Leadership series emphasized four basic principles of Leadership that seem very simplistic on the surface, but are extremely profound and powerful concepts and principles. We now refer to them as the "Four Absolutes of Leadership."

FOUR ABSOLUTES OF LEADERSHIP

1. Maintain Self-Esteem

2. Focus on Behavior

3. Encourage Participation

4. Listen to Motivate and Communicate

> **Whenever we attack someone's self-worth, only one of two things will happen, either he/she will fight back or run away and hide. We call this the "fight or flight" syndrome.**

> **As soon as we observe a behavior, we make an inference about that behavior. This is normal and natural—the key is we should never act on our inference, we must act on the behavior.**

1. <u>Maintain Self-Esteem</u>: Self-esteem generally refers to an individual's sense of self-worth. Whenever we attack someone's self-worth, only one of two things will happen, either he/she will fight back or run away and hide. We call this the "fight or flight" syndrome. Nothing beneficial or constructive ever comes from either of these situations. It is important to understand what we do to enhance one person's self-esteem may or may not work for someone else. The converse is also true, what we did to damage one person's self-esteem may or may not damage someone else's self-esteem. Every individual is different. We must get to know people on a personal level to really understand how our actions affect other people. Leaders must maintain people's self-esteem regardless of the situation.

2. <u>Focus on Behavior</u>: This absolute ties nicely into our discussions of behavioral expectations and is a key leadership principle. It is also the most difficult to get leaders to understand. The key issue is that, as soon as we observe a behavior, we make an inference about that behavior. This is normal and natural—the key is we should never act on our inference, we must act on the behavior. For example, if we see someone came to work late three times last week, we may infer that the person is lazy, has a bad attitude, and does not care about the job. When we approach this person about the tardiness, we may get upset and tell the person they have a bad attitude. We have attacked their self-esteem and violated the first principle of leadership. This person may fire back and attack you or run away and hide. No good will come from this scenario.

However, if we approach the individual and state the observable behavior, "I observed you coming to work late three times last week, what is going on?" we may get a completely different response or reaction. We may find out that the person has an ailing parent who needs assistance first thing in the morning. We may also find out the person stays late every evening to make sure the team does not suffer from the tardiness. Or we may find out that they do have a bad attitude. Please note that a leader is in the most powerful position when they have firsthand, observable information. Never rely on secondhand information. Stay focused on the behavior, good or bad, and do not act on your inferences.

> **A leader is in the most powerful position when they have firsthand, observable information.**

3. Encourage Participation: This absolute fits neatly into our leadership principle of empowerment. Do not solve problems or provide solutions for your people. In the above example, we may find that the person is just having problems getting organized in the morning so they can be at work on time. A good leader may probe and investigate what they think should be done to rectify the situation. The response could be explored and an action plan put in place. It would then be necessary to follow-up on the agreed upon action plan.

4. Listen to Motivate and Communicate: Good leaders listen more than they speak. Leaders know that they will never learn anything if they are doing all the talking. Learning to listen to the voices of your customers, processes (your people), and your suppliers will enhance people's self-esteem and promote communication. When you really focus on someone and actively listen to what they have to say, you are communicating to the person that you value their opinion. This in turn enhances people's self-esteem.

> **Good leaders listen more than they speak.**

√ *Lean Overview*

Great two-way communication is the ongoing investment a Leadership Team must make in its people

Communication

Understand that there is no teamwork in any organization without communication. When Leadership Teams are surveyed, 99 percent say that teams and teamwork are important to the success of their organization. Yet these same organizations have few, if any, successful teams. Teams—easy to say, but hard to do! Or is it?

As previously noted, the four elements required for teamwork to develop in an organization are:

1) High levels of two-way communication

2) Team members with diverse backgrounds

3) Common purpose/motivated by mission

4) Common goals/measurements

While Leadership Teams "mouth" the need for teams and teamwork, their actions against these requirements indicate something different.

For a team to develop and be successful, everyone in the organization must have a copy of the playbook. This is the importance of doing this 10-step Policy Deployment. This deployment, like a team playbook, outlines the organization goals (win the Super Bowl) and the activities (plays) that the team must execute to achieve the goals. The team has measurement systems (scoreboard) to track progress. The quarterback and coaches (Leadership Team) are constantly communicating verbally and visually with the team and sub-team members (offensive line, defense, special teams, etc.). The team makes adjustments along the path to the goal. One can only imagine the results of a football play where the quarterback only communicated the "play call" to two team members instead of all ten in the huddle. Yet this is most often the norm for Leadership Teams in American business.

Based on our experience running many organizations from the general manager and plant manager level, we have learned and believe this: 98 percent of people in organizations want to take care of their customers, they want the company to be successful, and they want to have jobs at the company in the future. To access these resources, an environment (culture) must be created where these 98 percent know they are valuable members of the team. The question for Leadership Teams and managers is: Do you want six to eight managers trying to achieve the company's budget, plans and goals, or do you want the entire organization doing that?

> At the management "report out" of a recent Kaizen Event, a 30-year company employee told management how pleased he was at getting the opportunity to participate in the event. "For 30 years the company has paid me to use my arms and my legs to do my job—and if they would have asked—they could have had my brain for free."

Without this Leadership Team communication, people in most organizations will learn about what is going on through the "rumor mill." Change is discovered, not announced. Remember, a rumor's sole purpose in life is to fill in voids in communication. Generally, the rumor mill is the most reliable way of obtaining information when the Leadership Teams fails to effectively communicate. People know when change is in the wind. They see management going to off-site meetings and get in-

√ Lean Overview

If Lean is the engine to becoming a World Class Enterprise, then communication is the fuel

volved in different types of training. Managers and supervisors come back from these events speaking a different language and acting differently.

If management does not effectively communicate the vision for the future and the impact that change is going to have on the organization and the people, then confusion and rumors ensue (as depicted in the model shown in Figure #23).

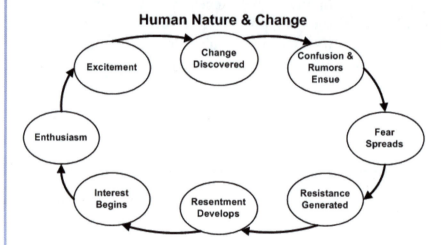

Figure #23

Confusion and rumors begin to spread fear in the organization and resistance begins to develop. It now takes a great deal of effort to change or overcome the resentment that has set in. In some organizations, management is never able to change or recover from the resentment that has occurred.

Figure #23 repeats itself every time a change is discovered and not announced

An effective Leadership Team can short circuit this confusion, fear, resistance, and resentment loop by announcing the change and communicating it to everyone at the same time. Then by communicating, communicating, and communicating about the change, the Leadership Team can begin to develop interest from the organization in the change (see Figure #24). The Leadership Team must continue to grow this interest, enthusiasm, and excitement by ongoing communication updates to the vision and the plan for what the organization will look like one, three, and five years down the road.

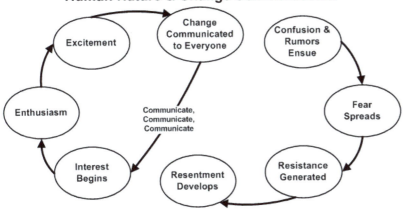

Figure #24

It is important to remember that the communication from all Leadership Team members must be honest and consistent. When the Leadership Team "breaks the huddle," every team member must be reading from the same page. Leadership Team trust violations will greatly impede or destroy the Policy Deployment effort. The organization is not expecting the Leadership Team to be perfect (mistake free), but it is expecting the team to be honest.

Empowerment

Once the team members know what part of the play (from the playbook) they must accomplish for the team to be successful, empowerment allows them to use 100 percent of their creativity, skills, and knowledge in doing their job without fear of retribution or second guessing by management.

Empowerment is not something we do to another person. The best we can do, as leaders, is to provide an environment where empowerment can occur. Leaders cannot just announce or proclaim that people are now empowered. They must be proactive in establishing an environment conducive to an empowered workforce. Here are cultural elements of an empowering environment:

- Associates are recognized as the organization's most valuable resource

- Teamwork is utilized throughout the organization

- Decision making is delegated

- Openness, initiative, and risk taking are promoted

- Accountability, credit, responsibility, and ownership are shared (here ownership means psychological ownership, not stock certificate ownership)

It is important to understand that associate empowerment is an evolutionary process not a revolutionary one.

The most important resource an organization has is its people!!

Teamwork

With communication, and the empowerment evolution that follows, in place, it is now possible to close the loop on the three remaining elements (from page 68) for teamwork to occur in an organization:

2) Team members with diverse backgrounds

3) Common purpose/motivated by a mission

4) Common goals/measurements

The most creative, best problem solving teams are those with team members that have diverse backgrounds. Diversity allows the composite team to view problems/opportunities from many angles or facets—a 360 degree global view. Every person working on a problem sees the problem from "their angle," facet, or frame of reference. This angle is determined by the person's background, education, experiences, and culture (BEEC). These factors force a person into viewing the problem from that angle or frame of reference. If there are 10 people on a team (or think of it as 9 clones of the same person) and they all have similar BEEC factors, great or even good creativity or problem solutions will not occur because the problem/opportunity is not seen in its entirety. Will the similar BEEC team come up with a solution? Yes. Will it ultimately in time be viewed as a good solution? No.

American organizations have a mixed bag on diversity. Fortune 1000 firms that work and compete in the global economy learned first that diversity was required to do business globally. They then learned that this diversity brought power to their teams. For companies of 500 people or less, which represent greater than 95 percent

Lean Overview

of all American businesses, it's a different story. When the President, CEO, or plant manager of these organizations are asked whether they have diversity in their workforce the answer will be yes. True enough, but there is no power (only untapped power) in this type of diversity. This diversity is based on hiring members of one or more local ethnic groups who will work for the wages being paid. In general, English communication skills are not a job requirement. Without communication there is no teamwork, and therefore no "diversity power." The largest type of waste (of the eight) in these organizations is #8, underutilized human resources.

Required elements #3 (common purpose/motivated by a mission) and #4 (common goals/measurements) are usually lumped together. In the Introduction, we discussed some of the barriers to doing Policy Deployment:

"The lack of Lean 'system thinking' is one of them. We broadly define the system as the processes required from the time the customer places the order for a product or service until the service is performed or the product ships. For customer satisfaction to occur, everyone in the organization must have customer satisfaction as a common goal so they all will pull in the same direction (a common goal is one of the four requirements for teamwork to occur). System thinking requires that all decisions and improvements in an organization are made based on their impact on the 'system efficiency.' If a suggested improvement will improve department efficiency but will negatively impact the system efficiency, it is not done."

Lean drives the authority, responsibility, and accountability down to the lowest levels in the organization. It is also the elimination of silos and departmentalization that are a traditional part of most corporate cultures so the flow of information and material through the organization can improve. An organization that is organized in silos or departments creates many handoffs. Wherever there are handoffs, there are delays and opportunities for errors.

In a World Class Enterprise, flexible, cross-functional teams are created to focus on processes that provide products or services to particular customers or markets from "quote to cash." These "Value Streams" or "Business Units" are assigned to a team leader who forms a team. The team is then given the autonomy to manage their own processes based on the organizational goals. The teams are focused on providing quality products or services, on-time, at a competitive price.

√ Lean Overview

Putting It All Together:

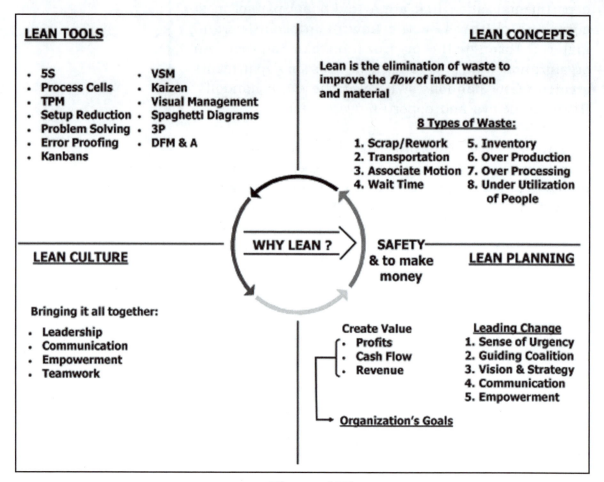

Figure #25
The Four Components of Lean

We have now come full circle: back to the Lean Planning component (See Figure #25). During the Lean Planning process we will start by identifying the key/core/critical projects that must be completed in a timely fashion to propel the organization to a new level of performance. These projects or opportunities will be goal oriented and linked directly to the business objectives of the organization.

Identifying these opportunities is only part of the planning process. In the planning process, we must also identify what we must do as an organization to develop the culture we need to support the project teams and all the supporting systems. This is Step 7. We may need to develop and implement a communication plan so the Leadership Team has a means to communicate the vision and the direction the organization is going. We may need to provide Lean training for our people so they will understand the Lean principles before meeting in teams. We may need to develop our own internal Lean Masters to facilitate teams to get the quantifiable results we expect. We may need to develop and implement a metrics system for the organization to show the improvements. We may need to provide leadership training for everyone who supervises people.

The list goes on and on. This is why the Leadership Team must understand what is involved in the four components of Lean prior to developing the Lean Implementation Plan in Step 7. As you progress through this book, you will discover a step-by-step Policy Deployment approach to developing and implementing a comprehensive Business Plan using Lean as the system for making improvements. This proven approach will improve any business. If taken seriously, this technique will make your organization World Class.

10 STEPS TO SUCCESSFUL POLICY DEPLOYMENT

1. Establish a Mission and Guiding Principles
2. Develop Business Goals
3. Brainstorm for Opportunities to Achieve Goals
4. Define Parameters to Value Opportunities
5. Establish Weighting Requirements, Rate Opportunities, and Prioritize
6. Conduct a Reality Check
7. Develop Lean Implementation Plan
8. Develop Bowling Chart
9. Countermeasures
10. Conducting Business Reviews

Step 1:

Establish a Mission and Guiding Principles

STEP 1 OBJECTIVE

Develop the outline/boundaries for the new organizational Lean Culture by:

- **Establishing/reiterating a clear concise Organizational Mission Statement that will focus and aid all associates in decision making**

- **Providing all associates with a list of "Organizational Guiding Principles and Behavioral Expectations"**

√ *Step 1*

10 Steps to Successful Policy Deployment

1. **Establish a Mission and Guiding Principles**
2. Develop Business Goals
3. Brainstorm for Opportunities to Achieve Goals
4. Define Parameters to Value Opportunities
5. Establish Weighting Requirements, Rate Opportunities, and Prioritize
6. Conduct a Reality Check
7. Develop Lean Implementation Plan
8. Develop Bowling Chart
9. Countermeasures
10. Conducting Business Reviews

The Mission Statement

The single greatest characteristic of a good leader is the ability to create a vision for the future. What will the company need to look like in one, three, and five years to still be competitive and growing? The leader must then be able to work with the people to establish a plan that will make it happen. This vision and plan must be communicated over and over again.

It can be easily noted that in this book the terms "Mission" and "Vision" are used almost interchangeably.

While "semi-strict" definitions exist,

Vision – A sensible and appealing picture of the future (Kotter)

Mission – Defines the business at its most basic level, who your company is, what you do, what you stand for, and why you do it (Tim Berry)

most organizations are either confused about the difference or they define the terms differently. It is important that organizations do not get hung-up on definitions. They must not get bogged down in semantics. The important concept here is for the Leadership Team to create a picture of where the organization will be at some point in the future and then, as Joel Barker would say, "build bridges" to the future.

The best example of visionary leadership is President John F. Kennedy's special address to Congress on the importance of space travel on May 25, 1961.

"I believe that this nation should commit itself to achieving the goal, before this decade is out, of landing a man on the Moon and returning him safely to the Earth. No single space project in this period will be more impressive to mankind, or more important for the long-range exploration of space; and none will be so difficult or expensive to accomplish. We propose to accelerate the development of the appropriate lunar space craft. We propose to develop alternate liquid and solid fuel boosters, much larger than any now being developed, until certain which is superior. We propose additional funds for other engine development and for unmanned explorations—explorations which are particularly important for one purpose which this nation will never overlook: the survival of the man who first makes this daring flight. But in a very real sense, it will not be one man going to the Moon—if we make this judgment affirmatively, it will be an entire nation. For all of us must work to put him there."

The intent of this Policy Deployment & Lean Implementation Planning book is to stimulate a discussion amongst the Leadership Team on where they want the organization to be or look like one, three, and five years down the road. This ten-step roadmap will be the mechanism the Leadership Team will use to build a bridge to the future. As Larry Rubrich so boldly states in the introduction that, "Lean in the hands of an organization's associates can make any required improvement or solve any business problem," then Lean and this 10-step roadmap can achieve any desired future state.

√ *Step 1*

Step 1 in Policy Deployment is for the company to have a clear, concise Mission Statement that will provide focus and aid in decision making.

One of Steven Covey's, *Seven Habits of Highly Effective People* is to *"Begin with the end in mind"*.

> *"When we begin with the end in mind, we have a personal direction to guide our daily activities, without which we will accomplish little toward our own goals. Beginning with the end in mind is part of the process of personal leadership, taking control of our own lives.*
>
> *"Organizational mission statements should be developed by everyone in the organization. If there is no involvement in the process, there will be no commitment to the statement. The reward system must compliment and strengthen the stated value systems.*
>
> *"An organization may have an all-encompassing mission statement, and each location, or even each team, may have their own. However, they should all dovetail with each other.*
>
> *"If the mission statements of your family and organization dovetail with your personal mission statement, and you use those statements to keep your end in mind, you will accomplish your goals more quickly and easily."*

Most companies already have a vision or mission statement; everyone is doing it, so it must be the right thing to do. But when we start working with various companies, we find out during our assessment process that

Establish A Mission and Guiding Principles

very few people can tell us what the mission statement is or how it applies to them. The primary reason for this is that they had no involvement in developing the vision nor was it communicated by senior management at every possible opportunity.

Robert Ayers (President of Goulds Pump and later promoted to President of the Fluid Technology Corporation all within ITT Industries) is one of the most visionary leaders the author has ever had the privilege to work with. When Bob first took over Goulds Pumps in 1998, they defined their mission as being the best pump company in the United States. It was not until they redefined their mission as being a global company that provides solutions in moving fluids, that they made significant improvements in the way they did business and presented themselves to the marketplace.

> *"The Industrial Products Group [Goulds Pump] will be the leader in fluid technology solutions to the global industrial marketplace. Our customers will recognize us as a provider of innovative services, systems, and products. Through creativity, operational excellence, and exceptional co-workers, we will grow our business and create shareholder value."*

This Mission Statement was developed by a cross-functional team. They defined "leader" by percent market share, operating income, and free cash flow. The team now understood that they were to develop a plan that would allow Goulds Pump to go international; we developed strategies that would take the organization to Europe, Middle East, and Asia. This Mission Statement also drove the organization to expand its business from the core. They now were in the business to provide valves and other related products that would control the move-

√ Step 1

ment of fluids. Goulds Pump was no longer a pump company, but a company that would provide solutions—in its service, systems, and product sectors.

An additional example of a Vision/Mission Statement is shown in Figure #26. Note that the St. Camillus' Vision Statement, like the ITT Mission Statement on page 83, answers the following questions:

- How will it affect our clients/customers?

- How will it affect our organization?

- How will it affect our co-workers?

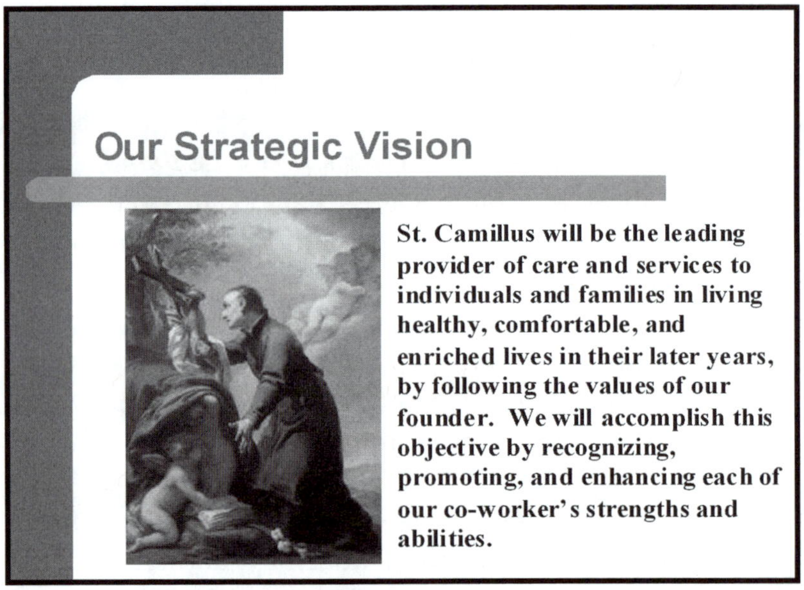

Our Strategic Vision

St. Camillus will be the leading provider of care and services to individuals and families in living healthy, comfortable, and enriched lives in their later years, by following the values of our founder. We will accomplish this objective by recognizing, promoting, and enhancing each of our co-worker's strengths and abilities.

Figure #26

You can now see how developing and communicating a clear Mission Statement can drive the decision-making process within an organization. It provides a focus and a direction. People could more easily stay focused on what they are doing rather than going back to management for permission to do something. They know where the company is going and they can now spend more time on getting things done which creates a bias for action.

Some guidelines in developing Mission Statements are:

- Short (3-5 sentences)

- Answers the questions: How will it affect our customers, the organization, and our associates?

- May comment on customers, markets, core values, organizational culture, ethics, etc.

SWOT Analysis & Core Competencies

At this time it is also worth conducting a SWOT analysis and discussing a company's core competencies.

We will not go into detail on how to conduct a SWOT Analysis (Strengths, Weaknesses, Opportunities, & Threats) by Products, Customers, and Markets. Most organizations can do this on their own. There is a tab in the plan on the CD where the Leadership Team can conduct this exercise as well as generate a discussion on what they believe to be their core competencies. Follow the brainstorming rules (found in Step 3) for this discussion.

From *Profit From the Core*, by Chris Zook with James Allen:

> "Few companies grow and create value sustainably over periods even as short as ten years. Those that do so tend to focus on one, or at most two, core businesses in which they are clearly the leader or, in the rare

√ Step 1

cases of the strong followers, in which they manage to simulate the economic conditions that accrue to market leadership. These economic conditions and market power give companies higher profitability, greater control over the extended industry profit pool, and tighter control over investable capital in their competitive arenas. Typically, as in the obvious cases of Coca-Cola, Anheuser-Busch, Intel, and Microsoft, the continued application of economic leadership leads first to growth that outstrips that of others in the industry and then to "traditional" scale leadership. For instance, two-thirds of our sustained value creators grew more rapidly than their industry averages and were thereby gaining share in their marketplaces. In fact, the average sustained value creator in our database grew twice as rapidly as its industry in revenues and more than three times as rapidly in total profits. The question naturally arises, then since most companies are followers, how can they gain market power and simulate leadership economics?

"Throughout the discussions of sustained value creation, we have indicated our strong belief that many companies have, or once had the right ingredients but somehow failed to recognize the potential of their profitable core. This failure has led companies to underinvest in the core, to set performance targets that are too low (leading to undermanagement), or to abandon the core prematurely for seemingly greener pastures in new or hotter industries."

A company that we have worked with manufactures various types of gears. During a discussion of its core competency, they stated that it was the machining of bevel gears. After a brutally honest discussion, they had to admit that their core competency was not the machining of bevel gears. However, what they needed to be World Class in was the ability to introduce new products into their manufacturing process which included the meticulous traceability of all manufacturing operations.

They needed to be able to ensure that, when a job was ready to be released to the shop, they had correctly identified all the tooling, gauging, fixturing, CNC programming, heat treating, and plating specifications; in other words, that the machine operators had everything they needed including the knowledge of how to properly process the product.

They also needed to be able to establish effective traceability of manufacturing operations without creating huge delays in the process. There were frequent delays in manufacturing because operators were looking for things, including information to run the job, or waiting for inspection or engineering. This discussion opened many people's eyes and they began to see the waste that was created by their own inefficiencies.

This discussion helps set the stage for the brainstorming session in Step 3. It helped the Leadership Team understand where they could take advantage of significant opportunities to start their company down the path of becoming World Class.

√ *Step 1*

Guiding Principles & Behavioral Expectations

In their book, *Control Your Destiny or Someone Else Will,* authors Noel Tichy and Stratford Sherman discuss how Jack Welch of GE characterized, measured, and dealt with the four types of leaders.

> *"The outside world finally began to understand GE's long obsession with values when the company released its 1991 annual report. In his chairman's letter, Welch repackaged one of his oldest ideas in a way that suddenly riveted the attention of business people around the world. He defined the four types of executives:*
>
> *'The first is one who delivers on commitments—financial or otherwise—and shares the values of the Company. His or her future is an easy call. Onward and upward. (Figure #27, Upper Right)*
>
> *'The second type of leader is one who does not meet commitments and does not share our values. Not as pleasant a call, but equally easy. (Lower Left)*
>
> *'The third is one who misses commitments but shares the values. He or she usually gets a second chance, preferably in a different environment. (Upper Left)*
>
> *'Then there's the fourth type—the most difficult for many of us to deal with. That leader delivers on commitments, makes all the*

88

numbers, but doesn't share the values we must have. This is the individual who typically forces performance out of people rather than inspires it: the autocrat, the big shot, the tyrant. Too often all of us have looked the other way—tolerated these "type 4" managers because "they always deliver"—at least in the short term. (Lower Right)

'And perhaps this type was more acceptable in easier times, but in an environment where we must have every good idea from every man and woman in the organization, we cannot afford management styles that suppress and intimidate. Whether we can convince and help these managers to change—recognizing how difficult that can be—or part company with them if they cannot, will be the ultimate test of our commitment to the transformation of this Company and will determine the future of the mutual respect and trust we are building. We know now that without leaders who "walk the talk," all of our plans, promises, and dreams for the future are just that—talk.'"

√ *Step 1*

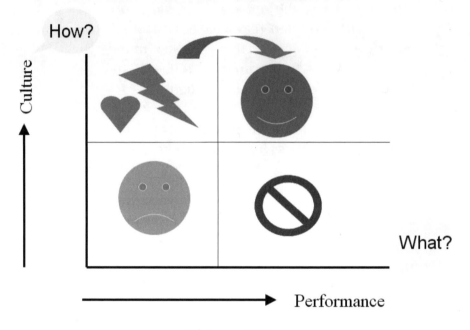

Figure #27

Figure #27 is a chart that was developed based on Jack Welch's definition of performance and values. The "X" axis is based on performance. How well you do your job? The "Y" axis is based on how you get work done (values/culture). The authors generally equate this to the traditional used car salesperson. His job is to sell cars. You could easily measure how many cars he sells and at what profit margin. But how he sells cars is just as important. He could lie and try to cheat you by telling you that the car has features that it really does not, or that it was driven by a little old lady once a week to church (down hill both ways) or he can be truthful and honest.

Most organizations do a good job in identifying "Personal Performance Metrics" (such as a Project Manager who completes a project on-time and within budget, a salesperson who hits his sales objective for the year, etc.). However, most organizations do a very poor job of identifying and measuring behavioral characteristics (empowerment, communications, etc.). In the lower left quadrant are those people whose performance is unacceptable and who will never fit into the Lean culture we are trying to create.

In the upper right quadrant are your high potential people—the people you plan to build the company upon. However, where do we tend to spend the most time? Most organizations spend most of their time dealing with the problem people in the lower left quadrant, when they should be spending time developing high potential people. If we do not spend time developing our good people they will leave. They will become disenchanted and find more rewarding work elsewhere.

In the upper left quadrant are those people who have the heart and desire to fit into the Lean culture but whose performance is still unacceptable. Work with these people. They may be in the wrong job, lack training, are uninspired, etc. Help them into the upper right quadrant. We want our people to be in the upper right quadrant. We want people who fit into the new Lean culture and are achieving the results necessary to meet the business objectives of the organization.

Jack Welch will tell you that the most difficult quadrant of all is the lower right quadrant. Most organizations are very reluctant to do anything about those people who do not want Lean to be successful. They will do whatever is necessary to undermine this process. They do not want to empower their people, they want to keep all the power to themselves (generally because they have all the process knowledge and are unwilling to share this knowledge). In fact, these people like firefighting; they will sometimes start fires just so they can go out and solve problems. They want to show everyone how important they are and how much they are needed—give these people 90 days to change their behavior. But before people can change their behavior they must understand what behavior they are currently exhibiting that is unacceptable and what the organization's desirable behavioral characteristics are.

Whenever the authors present this at a workshop, everyone is either trying to figure out where they think they are in the matrix or they can think of people that fit into each quadrant. The problem is that most companies do a relatively good job in defining the characteristics along the "X" axis, but fail to define the observable characteristics along the "Y" axis.

Do you really believe that people should maintain a safe, clean, and well organized workplace? Do you really believe that people should be empowered to make decisions involving their own work process? Do you really believe that people should be cross trained so we can have a flexible workforce? If you do, then you had better say so in observable and quantifiable terms. People need to understand that this is HOW work will get done in your organization.

As was mentioned in the leadership section of the Lean Overview, the Leadership Team can jump-start the culture change process by issuing organizational behavioral guidelines or guiding principles. Guiding principles or codes of conduct are short statements, usually printed on a laminated pocket card. These statements are "a set of rules or standards" that members of the organization use to guide their behavior and actions. Guiding principles define the "Y" axis on the chart in Figure #27.

These guiding principles or behavioral expectations should then be integrated into job descriptions, the new associate orientation program, and performance reviews.

As noted, the required culture change will occur only if these guiding principles are modeled by the Leadership Team all the time. Everything the Leadership Team says or does sends a message. As a wise leader once said "if you can't stand the heat," stay off the Leadership Team.

√ Step 1

> *Several years ago we were helping a small organization (< 100 people) implement Lean. We spent extra time working with the Leadership Team because in our initial organizational assessment, lack of trust in the Leadership Team came out in our interviews with company associates. The company associates wanted to help improve the company, but were hesitant to believe the Leadership Team was actually prepared to start "doing things differently." Presented with a summary of the assessment concerns, the Leadership Team assured us that they were prepared to follow the organization's new codes of conduct so the necessary culture change would be supported. This was related to all the company associates in a Lean Kick-off meeting.*
>
> *Several months later and it was Christmas time. The president of the organization wanted to send some wine across state lines to a colleague via UPS. The shipping clerk informed the president that this was illegal (at the time). The president told the shipping clerk to lie and send it anyway. Within 20 minutes, this story spread throughout the entire facility reinforcing the workforce's lack of trust in the Leadership Team. The Lean implementation died and three years later it is still dead.*

Three additional examples of behavioral expectations/guiding principles are shown in Figures #28, #29, and #30. Note that "single word" expectations may require a more detailed explanation when the expectations are deployed to the workforce.

Establish A Mission and Guiding Principles √

St. Camillus' Behavioral Expectations

- Work Safely
- Keep Customers First
- Respect Others
- Be Accountable
- Communicate
- Keep Learning
- Be Positive
- Be a Good Listener
- Help Solve Problems
- Take Pride in What You Do
- Tell the Truth
- Work as a Team

Figure #28
Behavioral Expectations Example

EXPECTATIONS
- SAFETY
- QUALITY
- PRODUCTIVITY
- ATTENDANCE
- ATTITUDE
- DEPENDABILITY
- HOUSEKEEPING
- CONTRIBUTION

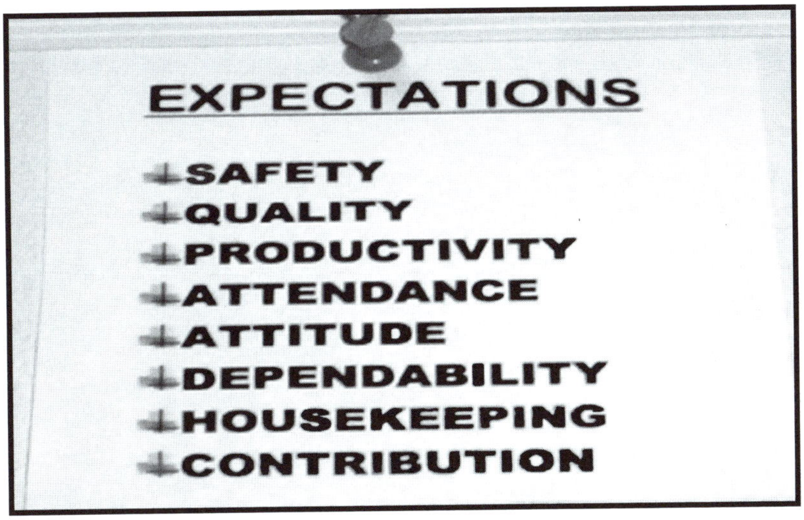

Figure #29
Behavioral Expectations Example

95

√ Step 1

Genie Industries Guiding Principles

Quality First
Quality for all our customers, internal and external, comes first. We will design and build in quality at the source, insuring 100% conformance to what we promise to our customers.

Customer Driven
We believe we exist because of satisfied customers, and we are dedicated to providing Full Customer Satisfaction over the long term. We will seek out, fully understand, and meet or exceed the needs of our customers.

Partnership with People
People are the key to our success. We are dedicated to the education, development, and involvement of all Genie Team Members.

Continuous Improvement
Continuous improvement is a part of everyone's job every day. We will seek out root causes, measure and visibly display performance information, and make decisions based on facts and data.

Cross Functional Management
We will treat each other with trust and respect and work together as an integrated, cross-functional team with a common goal of achieving Full Customer Satisfaction.

Organizational Alignment
Genie Management is responsible for aligning the company around a common vision and goals and providing the leadership, resources and support necessary to succeed.

Waste is Eliminated
We will do only those things that add value for our customers. Waste in all of its forms will be aggressively sought out and eliminated.

Superb Work Environment
We are committed to maintaining a superb work environment - safe, clean, well-organized, open and secure - to ensure that the highest quality products and services are produced for our customers.

Process Thinking
Reliable methods are developed and applied for all our organizational processes. We will continually seek out and standardize new and better methods.

Figure #30
Guiding Principles/Behavioral Expectations Example

Establish A Mission and Guiding Principles √

The best examples of behavioral expectations come from the grandfather of all quality gurus—W. Edwards Deming. Even though these 14 points were developed many years ago, they are just as relevant today as they were 50 years ago. Any organization that patterns its "behavioral expectations" after Deming's 14 points will not be disappointed.

1. Create constancy of purpose toward improvement of product and service, with the aim to become competitive and stay in business, and to provide jobs.

2. Adopt the new philosophy. We are in a new economic age. Western management must awaken to the challenge, must learn their responsibilities, and take on leadership for change.

3. Cease dependence on inspection to achieve quality. Eliminate the need for inspection on a mass basis by building quality into the product in the first place.

4. End the practice of awarding business on the basis of price tag. Instead, minimize total cost. Move towards a single supplier for any one item, on a long-term relationship of loyalty and trust.

5. Improve constantly and forever the system of production and service, to improve quality and productivity, and thus constantly decrease cost.

6. Institute training on the job.

7. Institute leadership. The aim of supervision should be to help people and machines and gadgets to do a better job. Supervision of management is in need of overhaul, as well as supervision of production workers.

√ Step 1

8. **Drive out fear,** so that everyone may work effectively for the company.

9. **Break down barriers b**etween departments. People in research, design, sales, and production must work as a team, to foresee problems of production and in use that may be encountered with the product or service.

10. **Eliminate slogans, exhortations, and targets** for **the work force asking** for zero defects and new **levels of productivity.** Such exhortations only create adversarial relationships, as the bulk of the causes of low quality and low productivity belong to the system and thus lie beyond the power of the work force.

11. A. **Eliminate work standards (**quotas) on the factory floor. Substitute leadership.

    B. **Eliminate management by objective.** Eliminate management by numbers, numerical goals. Substitute workmanship.

12. A. Remove barriers that rob the hourly worker of his right to pride of workmanship. The responsibility of supervisors must be changed from sheer numbers to quality.

    B. Remove barriers that rob people in management and in engineering of their right to pride of workmanship. This means, *inter alia,* abolishment of the annual or merit rating and of management by objective.

13. Institute a vigorous program of education and self-improvement.

14. Put everyone in the company to work to accomplish the transformation. The transformation is everyone's work

Establish A Mission and Guiding Principles √

TEAM ACTION FOR STEP 1:

Load the Excel spreadsheet from the enclosed CD onto your computer. Click on the tab labeled "Mission and Guiding Principles." Have the team brainstorm the company's Mission Statement and Guiding Principles (see Step 3 if the team needs a refresher on the brainstorming process). Insert the results of this brainstorming session into the spreadsheet.

EXAMPLE

Mission:

"The Industrial Products Group will be the leader in fluid technology solutions to the global industrial marketplace. Our customers will recognize us as a provider of innovative services, systems, and products. Through creativity, operational excellence, and exceptional co-workers, we will grow our business and create shareholder value."

Guiding Principles:

- We will maintain a safe, clean, and organized working environment
- Promote open and honest communications between all team members
- Establish flexibility and teamwork throughout the organization
- We will operate with integrity in everything we do
- Create an empowered workforce that is focused on waste elimination—"War on Waste"

Step 2:

Develop Business Goals

STEP 2 OBJECTIVE

Develop/reiterate SMART business goals to which all associate and Lean tool activities will be aligned. SMART goals are:

- Specific
- Measurable
- Achievable
- Relevant
- Time dimensioned

√ *Step 2*

10 Steps to Successful Policy Deployment

1. Establish a Mission and Guiding Principles

2. **Develop Business Goals**

3. Brainstorm for Opportunities to Achieve Goals

4. Define Parameters to Value Opportunities

5. Establish Weighting Requirements, Rate Opportunities, and Prioritize

6. Conduct a Reality Check

7. Develop Lean Implementation Plan

8. Develop Bowling Chart

9. Countermeasures

10. Conducting Business Reviews

There are generally only three key metrics that we look at when we first go into an organization. What is your safety record, how profitable are you, and what is the status of your cash flow? The only thing that should be more important to a company than making money is the safety of its people. After safety, companies are in business to make money over the long term.

We generally do not emphasize revenue growth unless a company is already profitable. Why would any company grow a business that is not profitable?

Figure #31 shows a Fishbone, Ishikawa, or what's also referred to as a "Cause and Effect" diagram. Most often used as a problem solving tool (see Step 9), the Fishbone diagram also can be used to enhance a desired outcome or achieve a business goal. The desired outcome or business goal is placed in the mouth of the fish. In this case, it's to create more value thereby positively impacting the organization's financials. To understand how to create more value, it is necessary to understand the "causes" of how the organization currently creates value so those activities can be enhanced or more causes added. For example, if "increased revenues" is placed in the mouth of the fish as one of the organization's goals (or effect), the team can then discuss/brainstorm potential causes for increased revenues. Several factors that would cause that effect might be selling in new markets, additional services for current customers, or raising prices.

Develop Business Goals √

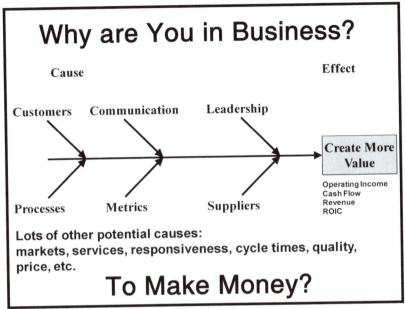

Figure #31

As noted in the Lean Overview chapter, the Leadership Team must establish high-level goals for the organization. In some cases, these goals have already been established by the Leadership Team or have been passed down to the Leadership Team from "Division" or "Corporate." Experience shows that for most companies of 500 people or less, formal goals that are shared with the entire organization do not exist outside the small group responsible for the budgeting/planning activity.

These "High-Level Business Goals" should focus on the business and strategic objectives and should be stated in the following format:

- ♦ We will improve our operating income from 8% to 12% in the next 12 months

√   Step 2

- We will increase the number of people we provide care for from 80 to 120 with the same resources within the next 18 months

- We will improve our inventory turns from 6 to 10 over the next 12 months

- We will grow our business through new products and services from $40M to $50M over the next 24 months

The Leadership Team must limit the number of goals. It is recommended that three to five goals be established. Remember—the fewer goals the better.

Company goals should be SMART goals.

- **S**pecific so there is no question whether or not things have improved

- **M**easurable so you can quantify the level of improvement (Remember: In God we trust, valid data required by everyone else)

- **A**chievable enough so they can really be accomplished; however, they must be stretch goals or not so easy they can be accomplished through "business as usual"

- **R**elevant to the direction of the business objectives and strategies

- **T**ime dimensioned so the time frame in which to accomplish the goal is known

It is normal for one or more of the organization's goals to be financial—but since Lean can solve any business problem, the true needs of the organization can be stated.

However, be cautious about setting "how to" objectives at this time. Frequently, organizations try to set objectives that are meant to solve a problem rather than to define a specific business goal. An objective such as "implementing a new ERP system across all facilities" is jumping to a solution and not focused on the true business objectives of the organization.

Also, be cautious about defining a goal just because it is someone's "pet" project. This may be a career limiting move to oppose the boss's pet project, but it must be done. Stay focused on the key business objectives of the organization. Remember—begin with the end in mind. How to achieve these business goals is defined in Step 3.

Breakthrough Goals and Objectives

Breakthrough objectives are stretch goals, "out of reach" of normal Daily Management (the day-to-day running of the company) but not "out of sight." Management should know what it looks like but not necessarily how to get there. It is okay to have one or two "Breakthrough" objectives that are strategic in nature. A Breakthrough objective such as penetrating a particular market, or developing and launching a certain number of new products may be appropriate.

Daily Management and a Word of Caution

Daily Management is the performance of business fundamentals in an organization required to serve customers and be profitable on a day-to-day basis. A World Class Enterprise can be built only on a strong foundation of an under-control workforce and processes. Lean and Lean improvements require the discipline of having procedures throughout the organization that all the associates follow. Likewise, Policy Deployment can be

---

10 STEPS TO SUCCESSFUL POLICY DEPLOYMENT

1. Establish a Mission and Guiding Principles

2. **Develop Business Goals**

3. Brainstorm for Opportunities to Achieve Goals

4. Define Parameters to Value Opportunities

5. Establish Weighting Requirements, Rate Opportunities, and Prioritize

6. Conduct a Reality Check

7. Develop Lean Implementation Plan

8. Develop Bowling Chart

9. Countermeasures

10. Conducting Business Reviews

√ *Step 2*

successful only when the daily business fundamentals are under control—those things that you do on a daily basis to serve your customer and run the business.

There are fifteen signs or symptoms of poor Daily Management:

1. Quality problems and incidents increase when vacation or other relief workers are employed

2. Process performance (quality and output) is noticeably and quantitatively different from shift to shift

3. Planned process changes/product changes do not go smoothly

4. Different operators run the same equipment differently

5. The same work rules, methods, and conditions have existed for a long time and things are not getting better

6. Process performance deteriorates with the age of equipment

7. Problems in key performance areas (e.g., quality, delivery, productivity) have been solved numerous times only to return after a short absence

8. Different departments (and individuals within departments) have or appear to have different goals and objectives associated with their outputs

9. Equipment failures and outages create havoc for the organization because dealing with them is almost always reactionary

10. Processes are run to the best of the operator's ability and adjustments and corrections are made based on judgment (as opposed to data)

11. When "seasoned" employees change jobs or retire, problems spring up in the area they left

12. Process performance modification and control is not documented empirically

13. Many problems of quality, traceability, and accountability are traced to between-shift transfer or handoff

14. Expedited orders slow down (even get lost) between shifts and/or between departments

15. When someone important is due to visit, you have to take special time and effort to clean and organize things

Before proceeding to Step 3, it would be wise for the Leadership Team to consider the status of the Daily Management discipline. Without the discipline of Daily Management, Lean, or any other type of improvements are not sustainable. These improvement efforts would then just be added to the organization's wasteful activities. See Figure #32 and #33. If the current level of Daily Management will not sustain improvements, then it is suggested that one of the goals of the first year Policy Deployment session be to develop Daily Management discipline.

√ *Step 2*

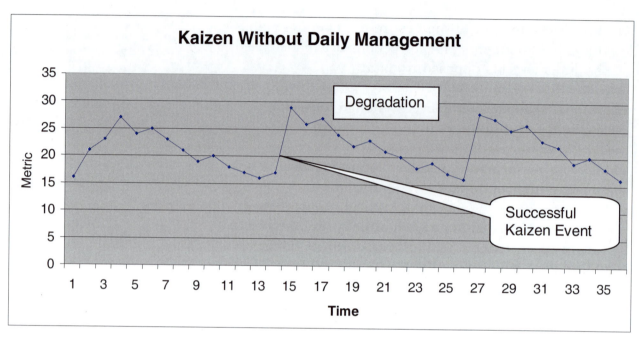

Figure #32

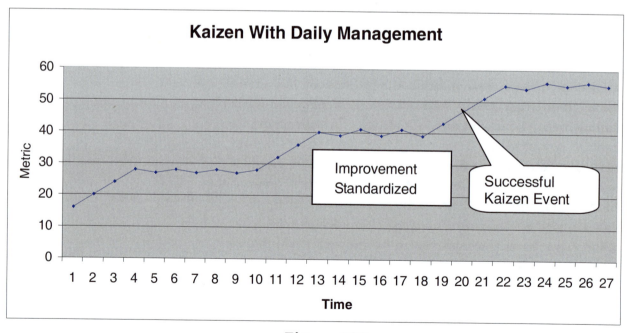

Figure #33

Develop Business Goals √

TEAM ACTION FOR STEP 2:

Load the Excel spreadsheet from the enclosed CD onto your computer. Click on the tab labeled "Business Goals." Have the team brainstorm the company's top three or four business goals (see Step 3 if the team needs a refresher on the brainstorming process). Remember safety should always be your number one goal and it should be zero. Insert the results of this brainstorming session into the spreadsheet.

EXAMPLE—HIGH-LEVEL BUSINESS GOALS

Goals must be SMART: Specific, Measurable, Achievable, Relevant, and Timely

1. Achieve 0 lost day injuries for next 12 months

2. Improve Net Income from 3% to 8% of sales by the end of the fiscal year

3. Improve Free Cash Flow from 30% to 70% of Net Income by the end of the fiscal year

4. Increase Revenues from $32 million to $36 million without eroding margins by the end of the fiscal year

Step 3:

Brainstorm for Opportunities to Achieve Goals

STEP 3 OBJECTIVE

Use the knowledge, experience, and ideas of the organization's workforce to brainstorm opportunities to achieve the Smart business goals. Begin the development of the workforce's "buy-in" to the implementation process.

√ *Step 3*

10 Steps to Successful Policy Deployment

1. Establish a Mission and Guiding Principles

2. Develop Business Goals

3. **Brainstorm for Opportunities to Achieve Goals**

4. Define Parameters to Value Opportunities

5. Establish Weighting Requirements, Rate Opportunities, and Prioritize

6. Conduct a Reality Check

7. Develop Lean Implementation Plan

8. Develop Bowling Chart

9. Countermeasures

10. Conducting Business Reviews

To fully utilize the resources assigned to brainstorm for opportunities to achieve the goals developed in Step 2, this brainstorming team, which includes the Leadership Team, should participate in at least a one-day *Lean Overview* training and a half-day session on *How to Prevent Lean Implementation Failures; 10 Reasons Why Failures Occur*. It is absolutely imperative that this team have a complete and thorough understanding of the four basic components of Lean (Lean Planning, Lean Concepts, Lean Tools, and Lean Culture) before beginning the brainstorming portion of this activity.

The reason for this is that the team must understand where all the waste elimination opportunities lie in order to achieve the stated business goals. Lean can solve any business problem, but before a plan can be developed to eliminate waste in your organization and solve the problem, you have to learn to see the waste.

Brainstorming is a critical step in the Policy Deployment process. A trained facilitator is required for this process to ensure that the team truly understands the rules for effective brainstorming so they can really identify all opportunities to achieve the goals. We know that many people think they understand the rules of brainstorming, but it is worth taking a moment here to review them.

√ *State problem in form of question*

Whenever possible state the idea in the form of a question. How can we reduce finished goods inventory from $2.0M to less than $750K? How can we reduce order entry from 3 days to 1 hour? How can we reduce the time to admit a patient in emergency from 3 hours to less than 10 minutes?

√ *Record all ideas on a flip chart and number them*

Have a skilled facilitator record all ideas on a flip chart and hang them all around the room. Do not get hung up on spelling things correctly—it is a very narrow mind that can spell something only one way. Use many different colors, to stimulate the creative thought process.

√ *Quantity of ideas most important*

It is not uncommon to generate 100 or more ideas. Do not be concerned if there is a lull in the generation of ideas. Just wait for the ideas to come. Maybe take a break, get some fresh air, and start the process up again.

√ *No criticism, discussion, or judgment allowed until all ideas have been presented. Clarification questions are okay.*

This is a tough one. This really requires a skilled facilitator. No one is to criticize someone else's idea —verbally or non-verbally. It is okay to ask clarifying questions so that the scope of the idea is understood, but do not analyze ideas at this time.

√ *Encourage participation by all*

We encourage participation by all by going around the room so everyone gets a chance to put an idea on the flip chart. This prevents the more outspoken people in the room from dominating the meeting and allows the more reserved individuals to participate. Only one idea can be given per turn and if a person does not have an idea when it is their turn they just say "pass."

√   **Step 3**

> √ *Piggyback—build on each other's ideas*
>
> It is desirable to piggyback your idea off of someone else's, but you have to wait your turn.
>
> √ *Don't limit thinking or imagination—thinking "outside the box" is required here!*
>
> It is easier to tame down a wild idea than to build up a bland idea. Let your imaginations run wild.
>
> √ *When all ideas have been presented, review each for feasibility and impact*

Safety will always be our number-one priority and will be an integral part of everything we do.

Once all the ideas have been generated it is time to evaluate them. The first thing the facilitator should do is identify any safety-related items. Safety will always be our number-one priority and will be an integral part of everything we do. If we identify a known safety issue during the brainstorming session, it is *not* put on the project list. Immediate threats require immediate action. The Leadership Team cannot knowingly let a safety issue exist. Any safety issues identified during the brainstorming session that pose an immediate threat to our associates must go directly onto a Kaizen Newspaper (Figure #34) where we identify the action item, who will be responsible for resolving the issue, and when the issue will be resolved. Longer term identifiable safety issues that focus on safety prevention like "upgrading the current fire alarm system with visual and audio cues," must go on the Safety Implementation plan.

Please note that under the "Who" column is the name of one of the members of the brainstorming team who will be responsible to ensure the action item will be completed. Normally a volunteer is requested. While this person can recruit other members of the organization to help them with this task, they are responsible for its completion. We call this, "One back to pat."

**Figure #34
Filling in the Kaizen Newspaper**

The facilitator should then begin to review the list of brainstormed ideas and lead the discussion on whether there are any ideas that are impractical. Maybe an idea would require too much capital, violates customer requirements, or is inconsistent with our overall strategies. If the entire group agrees that an idea is just not practical at this time, then take it off the list or put it on a "Parking Lot" list for later consideration (and to make sure the ideas do not get lost). The goal is to whittle down the brainstormed lists to only feasible ideas. Remember, the team will ultimately vote on the best ideas and this is the final whittling.

Next the brainstormed list is affinitized. This is where like ideas are consolidated/clustered together so that when the team votes for the best ideas in the next step,

√ Step 3

**Figure #35
Team Brainstorm List**

they will not use more than one vote to capture one good idea. For example, let's say on a team's brainstormed list of feasible ideas, idea #24 was to "reduce the time it takes to perform a financial close at the end of the month," and idea #67 was to "Value Stream Map the financial close process." Since the VSM tool works well at reducing lead times, these ideas both have the same goal and would be combined. Another example, idea #8 was to "reduce the operations inventory," and idea #85 was to "use Kanbans to control administrative supplies inventory." Again, these similar ideas that would both use Kanbans to control inventory could be combined.

Next, the team prioritizes the best ideas by voting. In multi-voting, we give each team member a set number of votes (usually 8-10% of total # of feasible ideas) that they can use to vote for the ideas they think will have the greatest impact on achieving the goals established in Step 2. Limiting the number of votes requires the team to focus on the ideas with the maximum improvement potential from their perspective. The voting is then done by secret ballot so as not to influence other people's opinions. The solutions with the greatest number of votes (ranked in order of number of votes) are the ideas the team will use to achieve the goals. Usually the top 20-30 vote-getting ideas go forward from here. At this time, the team will not know if there are enough or too many ideas until they complete Step 6—the Reality Check. Step 6 can be an iterative Step (check, adjust, then check again). This is where the "benefit" (from Steps 4 & 5) of all the "go forward" ideas are added or combined to assure that the goals from Step 2 will be reached.

To support the completion of Steps 4 and 5 later, the voted-for ideas must be scoped and clarified. "Scoping" an idea means all projects should be "sized" so they can be completed in three months. As noted previously, it is desirable that most improvement ideas be implemented in a Kaizen Event format which allows 90 days from event preparation to event completion. For example, idea #55 on the go-forward idea list is to implement Kanbans with all external suppliers. The current scope or size of this idea, depending on how many external suppliers the organization has, would probably make it very difficult to complete in 90 days. If the idea was rescoped to "Implement Kanbans with the top 5 suppliers," it can fit into the 90 day timeframe.

10 Steps to Successful Policy Deployment

1. Establish a Mission and Guiding Principles

2. Develop Business Goals

3. **Brainstorm for Opportunities to Achieve Goals**

4. Define Parameters to Value Opportunities

5. Establish Weighting Requirements, Rate Opportunities, and Prioritize

6. Conduct a Reality Check

7. Develop Lean Implementation Plan

8. Develop Bowling Chart

9. Countermeasures

10. Conducting Business Reviews

√ Step 3

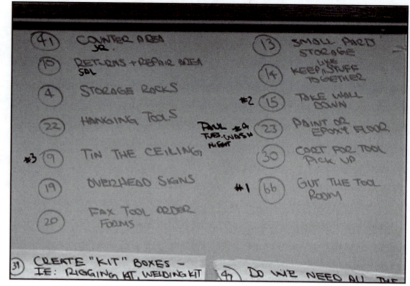

Figure #36
Voted for List, Top 13 Shown

Clarifying a project means determining "how much" or "how far" to take the improvement initiative the first time around. Remember, Lean requires continuous improvement which means no improvement project is ever totally completed—it just moves down the "achieving the organization's goals" priority list.

For example, if idea #33 on the go-forward list is to "improve the uptime on machine #4," how can that idea be valued in dollars or customer satisfaction? The value of the idea cannot be determined until we clarify this idea. For example, "reduce the change-over time on machine #4 by 75%" or "reduce the unplanned downtime on machine #4 by 50%."

Brainstorming is a powerful tool and a critical process to the success of Policy Deployment. It turns the organizations goals, which were only a dream when they were developed, into a plan. The more quality ideas the team can come up with, the better the results. The brainstorming process also facilitates asking the brainstorming team tough questions such as: Are we in the correct markets? How well are we managing our product portfolio? How profitable is each of our products/customers/markets? Is our structure in line with our strategies? Do we have too much corporate structure and associated overhead cost? This type of critical thinking may require that the team go back to Step 2 to review their business goals for revalidation.

We may want to conduct a SWOT (Strengths, Weaknesses, Opportunities, & Threats) Analysis, as well as, review our core competencies to better understand our strategic direction and to better identify opportunities to achieve the goals.

Team Action for Step 3:

Load the Excel spreadsheet from the enclosed CD onto your computer. Click on the tab labeled "Impact Analysis Worksheet." Have the team brainstorm as many ideas as possible to achieve the goals developed in Step 2. Scope each idea or opportunity so it can be accomplished within 90 days. Have the team multi-vote on the top 20 to 30 ideas. Insert the results (in # of votes sequence) of this brainstorming session into the spreadsheet. Also place the Business Goals from Step 2 into the "Benefit" section of the spreadsheet.

√ Step 3

EXAMPLE

BENEFIT		
	TOTAL BENEFIT	
	Revenue Growth	
	Cash Flow	
	Net Income	

#	BRAINSTORMED IDEAS/PROJECT DESCRIPTION
5	Reduce System Cycle Time (from quote to cash) from 67 days to 30 days
6	Reduce returns from 3% of sales to less than 1% of sales
8	Reduce scrap in the foundry from 6% to 3% of sales
9	Reduce set-up time on machine #4 from 3 hours to less than 30 minutes
10	Reduce finished goods inventory from $9M to less than $3M
11	Consolidate warehouses after reducing finished goods inventory
12	Reduce pricing errors from 9 per order to zero
13	Reduce turnover of key personnel from 3% to zero
14	Develop a process to respond to an RFQ in a single phone call

120

Step 4:

Define Parameters to Value Opportunities

STEP 4 OBJECTIVE

Evaluate and prioritize the brainstormed ideas/projects and opportunities. This valuation system must consider:

- Impact on the organization's goal(s)
- People resource requirements
- Capital expenditure requirements
- The risk that the idea/project cannot be completed

√ Step 4

10 Steps to Successful Policy Deployment

1. Establish a Mission and Guiding Principles

2. Develop Business Goals

3. Brainstorm for Opportunities to Achieve Goals

4. **Define Parameters to Value Opportunities**

5. Establish Weighting Requirements, Rate Opportunities, and Prioritize

6. Conduct a Reality Check

7. Develop Lean Implementation Plan

8. Develop Bowling Chart

9. Countermeasures

10. Conducting Business Reviews

At this point, we are preparing to evaluate each idea by the potential "Benefit" versus the potential "Effort" involved to complete each project.

The first thing the team must do is take the company's goals that were established in Step 2 and brainstorm what would be considered a low, medium, or high impact on each goal. For example, assume one of an organization's Step 2 goals was to improve operating income from 3% to 8% next year. The question becomes how much cost savings would need to be generated to support that level of operating income increase. If the team decides that a project with an impact of $50,000 or higher would have a significant impact on operating income, then the team may establish ranges such as:

♦ $0 to $20,000—low impact on operating income —score of 1

♦ $20,000 to $50,000—medium impact on operating income—score of 3

♦ Greater than $50,000—high impact on operating income—score of 5

If the goal of improving operating income from 3% to 8% represented a $2 million increase, then the dollar impacts shown in the above example are probably too low. Team consensus is required here.

For each project on the Impact Analysis Worksheet, the team must establish low, medium, and high impact for each "Benefit" to a project. Once again, these benefits go back to the business goals of the organization. This is a critical part of the planning process because it prevents the organization from working on the wrong projects or on the boss's "pet" project. This is the only way to take the "politics" out of the decision-making process.

The team must also establish low, medium, and high impact for each of the "Efforts" to complete each project. Generally, the "Effort" categories do not change. They consist of the estimated number of personnel and time required to complete a project, the estimated potential capital expenditure to complete a project, and the project risk. Of all the "Benefit" and "Effort" categories, the only one that is somewhat subjective is "Project Risk." Project Risk defines the probability the project will not be completed or will not work when completed. All other categories must be definitively defined. For example, we may end up with a project that will raise prices for Product "A" by 10%. This project may not be well-received by the customers and exceed market expectations. This project will most likely have more risk than reducing downtime on a machine or implementing inventory Kanbans.

For the Valuation Parameters example on page 125, the organization's four goals from Step 2 were:

- Achieve 0 lost day injuries for next 12 months

- Improve Net Income from 3% to 8% of sales by the end of the fiscal year

- Improve Free Cash Flow from 30% to 70% of Net Income by the end of the fiscal year

- Increase Revenue from $32 million to $36 million without eroding margins by the end of the fiscal year

√ *Step 4*

> ### TEAM ACTION FOR STEP 4:
>
> **Load the Excel spreadsheet from the enclosed CD onto your computer. Click on the tab labeled "Impact Analysis Worksheet." Scroll down to the section labeled "*Valuation Parameters.*" Have the team brainstorm, discuss, and come to a consensus on the Valuation Parameters. Insert the results of this brainstorming session into the spreadsheet.**

EXAMPLE

Valuation Parameters

GOALS:

Net Income
1 = Net Income impact of less than $25K
3 = Net Income impact of between $25K to $100K
5 = Net Income impact of greater than $100K

Cash Flow:
1 = $25K improvement in Cash Flow
3 = $25K to $50K improvement in Cash Flow
5 = Greater than $50K improvement in Cash Flow

Revenue Growth:
1 = Less than a 1% improvement in Revenue Growth
3 = 1% to 3% improvement in Revenue Growth
5 = Greater than a 3% improvement in Revenue Growth

RESOURCES REQUIRED & RISK

Resource requirements:
1 = 240 or fewer people hours. For example, 1 week Kaizen Event with 6 people (not including preparation & follow-up work)
3 = 240 to 520 people hours.
5 = More than 520 people hours.

Capital Expenditure Requirements:
1 = Less than $25K
3 = Between $25K and $100K
5 = Greater than $100K

Project Risk
1 = Low
3 = Medium
5 = High

Step 5:

Establish Weighting Requirements, Rate Opportunities, and Prioritize

STEP 5 OBJECTIVE

Rate and then prioritize for implementation the brainstormed ideas/projects and opportunities based on valuation system developed in Step 4.

√ *Step 5*

10 Steps to Successful Policy Deployment

1. Establish a Mission and Guiding Principles

2. Develop Business Goals

3. Brainstorm for Opportunities to Achieve Goals

4. Define Parameters to Value Opportunities

5. **Establish Weighting Requirements, Rate Opportunities, and Prioritize**

6. Conduct a Reality Check

7. Develop Lean Implementation Plan

8. Develop Bowling Chart

9. Countermeasures

10. Conducting Business Reviews

The next step is to establish a "weighting" for each of the "Benefits" and "Efforts" categories. This step is more critical than most people realize. Use the same three categories that were used in Step 4 under "Benefits": operating income, cash flow, and revenue growth. How the team "weights" each of these will have an impact on behaviors within the organization. Suppose the team establishes a weighting as follows:

- 30%   Operating Income
- 60%   Cash Flow
- 10%   Revenue Growth

What did the team communicate to the entire management team and the rest of the organization? That the organization should focus on anything that improves cash flow, such as reducing inventory, extending days payable, reducing days receivable, consolidating space (for example: eliminating the need for a warehouse), and reducing cycle times. People do not need to ask a lot of questions or seek permission. If they are not working on something to improve cash flow, they are working on the wrong thing. It does not mean that people are not going to do what they can to improve operating income. It does mean that if confronted with two improvement initiatives—one that improves cash flow and another that will improve operating income—we should choose the project that will improve cash flow over everything else (except safety).

Likewise the team needs to establish weighting criteria for the "Effort" side of the equation. The team needs to weight the importance of "personnel requirements," "capital expenditures," and "project risk." Personnel requirements and capital expenditures are examples of an organization's resources, which are not unlimited,

128

and may be available in an uneven supply. The amount of project risk a business can accept may reflect the organization's current financial position or its culture. Google Inc., the internet search engine, for example, accepts high levels of project risk because it knows that this culture is required to develop "cutting edge" technology.

Effort weighting can prevent an idea/project from reaching the final idea/project recommended priority list when the organization is unable to support it from a resources or risk standpoint.

If the team establishes a weighting as follows:

20%   Personnel Requirements

70%   Capital Requirements

10%   Risk

then the team has just communicated to the rest of the company's associates that spending money on capital equipment or capital improvements is not desirable. Remember that Lean focuses on low cost or no cost solutions. It also communicates to the rest of the organization that the team is willing to take risks at this time and that people resources are available to complete ideas/projects.

We now begin the "Valuing" part of the process. Once the team has the weighting criteria completed, they can begin the laborious task of assigning each idea/project a low (1), medium (3), or high (5) impact on each one of the project categories under "Benefits" versus "Effort."

√ *Step 5*

This task can be laborious because the team may have to spend some time discussing the impact of each project on each of the "Benefit" and "Effort" categories. This is why it is important to have finance involved in this process. If finance is not going to give you credit for project savings or it is not real savings and will not hit the bottom-line, then you cannot count it as a benefit. An example might be freeing up floor space. If we conduct a Kaizen Event that frees up a great deal of floor space, finance may not give us any credit for this project because there may not be any real savings that will hit the bottom-line. However, if we free up significant floor space and are able to consolidate inventory from a warehouse down the street that we are renting, then finance may give us credit in the form of no longer having to pay the rent on the warehouse, which would be real, hard-dollar cost savings.

We strongly recommend that every company read the book *Accounting for World Class Operations*, by Jerrold Solomon. This book is an excellent resource to aid in understanding the correlation between Lean and current financial reporting practices.

At this point, every group doing this process wants to get into problem solving. A skilled facilitator is required to keep the group focused on developing the plan and not solving problems. If you want an empowered workforce, let the people come up with the best solutions. They know the processes better than anyone in the room and will most likely come up with the most workable solutions. It is also easier to implement and sustain change when the people on the Kaizen teams come up with the solutions.

Now that all the ratings for all the ideas/projects have been established, they can be entered into the spreadsheet, at which time the spreadsheet will calculate the Total Benefit, Total Effort, Benefit/Effort, and the Benefit minus the Effort for each idea/project. The ideas/projects can then be sorted based on their overall impact (Benefits minus Effort or Benefits/Effort). It really does not make a big difference which you use. What we want to do is separate all the ideas/projects that will have a high impact on goals with a low consumption of resources. We call these projects "low hanging fruit." Projects that have medium to low impact on our goals with medium to high commitment of resources will be done at a later date or not at all.

Once there is a recommended list of projects it is up to the Leadership Team to make the final determination of what to do next. It is common to have "enabling projects" that are far down on the list but must be done before other projects can be completed. For each project, the team should ask if there are any known obstacles that will impede the project or prevent its completion. There might also be projects that our newly trained Lean Facilitators are not yet qualified to lead. There may be other considerations, but this tool does not replace the role of the Leadership Team and the eventual decision-making process. The Leadership Team must be responsible for establishing the priority and timing of each project.

What happens in most companies when they start to identify all these opportunities is that management wants all these projects done at once. They begin to see all the waste in their organization and they want it to go away now! When this happens, the project plan begins to look like Figure #37.

√ Step 5

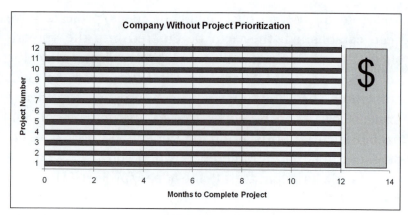

Figure #37

We have been in organizations like this one. People go to meetings once a week for an hour or two. Very little gets accomplished. People get discouraged and either start skipping meetings or stop going all together. There may be some financial impact after months and months of work.

World Class Enterprises Identify, Scope, Value, and then Prioritize projects as part of their Policy Deployment process. They stay focused on what is really important. Everyone in the organization knows that the people working on a Kaizen Event are working on the most important project going on in the company right now. They know that the only thing more important is safety and continuing to meet the customer requirements. Otherwise, this project has a specific goal and once the Kaizen team reaches this goal the company as a whole will be one step closer to achieving the business goals of the organization. The project plan then begins to look like that in Figure #38.

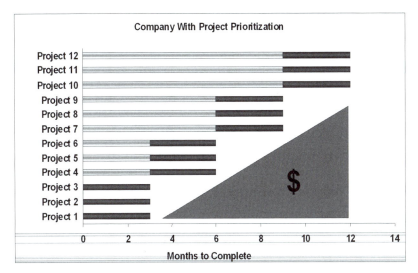

Figure #38

People start seeing the results of their efforts early on in the process. They start taking pride in their accomplishment and have a sense the company is on the right track. The company should provide rewards and recognition after each Kaizen team reaches its goal. Be sure to communicate, communicate, and communicate your successes—nothing breeds success, like success.

√ Step 5

Team Action for Step 5:

Load the Excel spreadsheet from the enclosed CD onto your computer. Click on the tab labeled "Impact Analysis Worksheet." Have the team brainstorm, discuss, and come to a consensus on the "Weighting" for each "Benefit" and "Effort" category. Then rate each project:

- **1 = Low**
- **3 = Medium**
- **5 = High impact**

in each of the categories. The facilitator can insert the results of this session into the spreadsheet as the team works through each idea/project. When all the ideas/projects have been rated, sort the projects by either Benefit/Effort or Benefit minus Effort to establish a recommended priority for Step 6.

Establish Weighting Requirements, Rate Opportunities, and Prioritize √

EXAMPLE

#	BRAINSTORMED IDEAS/PROJECT DESCRIPTION	BENEFIT - Net Income	BENEFIT - Cash Flow	BENEFIT - Revenue Growth	TOTAL BENEFIT	EFFORT - Personnel Requirements	EFFORT - Capital Expenditure Requirements	EFFORT - Project Risk (Low, Medium, High)	TOTAL EFFORT	Benefit / Effort	Benefit - Effort	RECOMMENDED PRIORITY
	Importance Weighting:	30%	60%	10%	100%	20%	70%	10%	100%			
1	Excellent Project …. low hanging fruit	5	5	5	5.0	1	1	1	1.0	5.0	4.0	
2	Mediocre Project	3	3	3	3.0	3	3	3	3.0	1.0	0.0	
3	Poor Project	1	1	1	1.0	5	5	5	5.0	0.2	-4.0	
4					-				-	0.0	0.0	
5	Reduce System Cycle Time (from quote to cash) from 67 days to 30 days	5	5	5	5.0	3	1	1	1.4	3.6	3.6	1
6	Reduce returns from 3% of sales to less than 1% of sales	5	3	3	3.6	3	1	1	1.4	2.6	2.2	3
8	Reduce scrap in the foundry from 6% to 3% of sales	5	1	3	2.4	3	1	1	1.4	1.7	1.0	4
9	Reduce set-up time on machine #4 from 3 hours to less than 30 minutes	5	1	3	2.4	3	1	1	1.4	1.7	1.0	5
10	Reduce finished goods inventory from $9M to less than $3M	1	5	1	3.4	1	1	3	1.2	2.8	2.2	2
11	Consolidate warehouses after reducing finished goods inventory	3	1	1	1.6	3	1	1	1.4	1.1	0.2	6
12	Reduce pricing errors from 9 per order to zero	3	1	1	1.6	3	1	1	1.4	1.1	0.2	7
13	Reduce turnover of key personnel from 3% to zero	3	1	1	1.6	3	1	1	1.4	1.1	0.2	8
14	Develop a process to respond to an RFQ in a single phone call	1	1	5	1.4	3	3	1	2.8	0.5	-1.4	9

135

Step 6:

Conduct a Reality Check

STEP 6 OBJECTIVE

To determine, if all the prioritized ideas/projects from Step 5 are fully achieved/implemented, will the goals established in Step 2 be reached?

√ Step 6

10 Steps to Successful Policy Deployment

1. Establish a Mission and Guiding Principles

2. Develop Business Goals

3. Brainstorm for Opportunities to Achieve Goals

4. Define Parameters to Value Opportunities

5. Establish Weighting Requirements, Rate Opportunities, and Prioritize

6. **Conduct a Reality Check**

7. Develop Lean Implementation Plan

8. Develop Bowling Chart

9. Countermeasures

10. Conducting Business Reviews

Step 6 compares the value of all of the prioritized ideas that the Leadership team has selected to work on in the current fiscal year (Step 5), when they are completed, to the organization's goals from Step 2. "When the ideas can be implemented," becomes the real question and requires a need for consensus. Knowing all projects cannot be completed at once, the question is: "How many quality projects can be launched in the first, second, and third quarter to achieve our business objectives for the year?" (See example of project timing on page 141.)

If the value of all the ideas meets or exceeds the organization's goals—congratulations! Move to Step 7. If they do not—read on.

This is the iterative part of Step 6. Check for goal attainment, make adjustments, check again.

At this point, short of projects to meet the goals, the team has several options from which to pick and eliminate the shortfalls:

♦ Revisit the list of "voted for" ideas. Are there ideas that were not moved forward to Step 4 that would eliminate the shortfalls?

♦ Move the implementation timing forward in time for certain ideas so the results for this year are greater. This may require hiring additional resources (skilled Lean Facilitators) or relying on outside consultants. Using outside consultants would only be necessary until the organization trains internal candidates.

♦ Conduct another brainstorming session for the shortfall area.

The team also must consider whether or not they have enough trained resources to lead teams. In Larry Rubrich's book, *How to Prevent Lean Implementation Failures, 10 Reasons Why Failures Occur*, the 7th reason is the "Lack of Lean Leadership." In this section of the book, it states that research conducted on World Class Enterprises has found that one percent of the total population must be trained, full-time, dedicated resources to the Lean initiative. Nothing else will work. Many companies try to shortcut this step. They try to find people who will work part-time as Lean facilitators and part-time in doing their old job. It never works. No matter how management tries to structure the new workload, their old jobs always take 100% of their time and consequently they end up doing Lean projects on their own time. Lean facilitators then end up becoming overworked and frustrated.

ITT Industries trained over 330 full-time Lean Facilitators and Champions in the first year without backfilling any positions. These people were full-time, dedicated resources. They represented 1% of the entire workforce worldwide. ITT had to trust that this commitment would pay off in the long run. It was a huge leap of faith for a relatively conservative organization, but it resulted in a highly successful Lean-Six Sigma implementation.

Management has to understand that this action is an investment in the company's future. What Lean will do is increase the capacity of your organization. At some point, the company will have to try to figure out what they are going to do with all the extra people anyway. You may as well begin by training your high potential people to work high impact projects.

√ **Step 6**

> TEAM ACTION FOR STEP 6:
>
> **Action Step 6: Load the Excel spreadsheet from the enclosed CD onto your computer. Click on the tab labeled "Conducting a Reality Check." Have the team brainstorm, discuss, calculate, and come to a consensus on whether or not the company has enough projects in queue and associated resources to achieve the business goals identified in Step 2. It is important that the team understands the timing of all projects. If, at this point, the team has not identified enough projects and resources to achieve the business objectives, they must:**
>
> ♦ **Go back to the brainstorming list of Step 3. Only the top 20-30 "voted for" ideas were moved forward to Step 5. Go further down on this list for more ideas to move forward.**
>
> ♦ **Figure out how to get more projects done earlier in the year**
>
> ♦ **Re-brainstorm for new ideas.**
>
> **This is the iterative part of Step 6. The facilitator can insert the results of this session into the spreadsheet as the team works through each project.**

EXAMPLE

#	Brainstormed Ideas/Project Descriptions which Support the High-Level Business Goals	Estimated Impact on Net Income	Estimated Impact on Cash Flow	Estimated Impact on Revenue Growth	Actual Impact on Net Income	Actual Impact on Cash Flow	Actual Impact on Revenue Growth
1	Reduce Total Cycle Time (from quote to cash) from 67 days to 30 days	$475,000	$200,000	$2,850,000			
2	Reduce returns from 3% of sales to less than 1% of sales	$175,000	$0	$350,000			
3	Reduce scrap in the foundry from 6% to 3% of sales	$210,000	$0	$0			
4	Reduce set-up time on machine #4 from 3 hours to less than 30 minutes	$185,000	$0	$0			
5	Reduce finished goods inventory from $9M to less than $3M	$60,000	$375,000	$0			
6	Consolidate warehouses after reducing finished goods inventory	$160,000	$0	$0			
7	Reduce pricing errors from 9 per order to zero	$145,000	$0	$0			
8	Reduce turnover of key personnel from 3% to zero	$105,000	$0	$900,000			
9	Develop a process to respond to an RFQ in a single phone call	$0	$0	$0			
10	Project 10	$0	$0	$0			
11	Project 11	$0	$0	$0			
12	Project 12	$0	$0	$0			
	Estimated Current Year Impact =	$1,515,000	$575,000	$4,100,000			
	Target =	$1,500,000	$500,000	$4,000,000			

Implementation Project Timing

	January	February	March	April	May	June	July	August	September	October	November	December
Project 1	A project started on January 1st and completed in 3 months may only have 9 months worth of impact											
Project 2												
Project 3												
Project 4				A project started on April 1st and completed in 3 months may only have 6 months worth of impact								
Project 5												
Project 6												
Project 7								A project started on July 1st and completed in 3 months may only have 3 months worth of impact				
Project 8												
Project 9												
Project 10										A project started on October 1st and completed in 3 months may not have any impact this year		
Project 11												
Project 12												

Step 7:

Develop Lean Implementation Plan

STEP 7 OBJECTIVE

Determine who is responsible, and what Lean activities must be accomplished to support or enable the full implementation of the prioritized ideas/projects from Step 5. These enabler activities may include:

- **Lean/Policy Deployment kickoff meetings**
- **Lean training**
- **Countermeasures training (Step 9)**
- **Organization-wide daily measurement systems**
- **Customer/Supplier meetings**
- **Communication systems**
- **Development of monthly all associates meeting**

√ *Step 7*

10 STEPS TO SUCCESSFUL POLICY DEPLOYMENT

1. Establish a Mission and Guiding Principles

2. Develop Business Goals

3. Brainstorm for Opportunities to Achieve Goals

4. Define Parameters to Value Opportunities

5. Establish Weighting Requirements, Rate Opportunities, and Prioritize

6. Conduct a Reality Check

7. **Develop Lean Implementation Plan**

8. Develop Bowling Chart

9. Countermeasures

10. Conducting Business Reviews

We have finally come to the point where we can start to put the plan together. People get tired of the old cliché, "plan your work and work your plan." But it is so true. It is amazing how many organizations do not have a detailed plan to achieve their business goals and objectives. It was Benjamin Franklin who said, "I have always thought that one man of tolerable abilities may work great changes, and accomplish great affairs among mankind, if he first forms a good plan, and, cutting off all amusements or other employments that would divert his attention, make the execution of that same plan his sole study and business."

The first things we put on the plan (see the *Lean Implementation Plan* tab on the included CD) are the ideas/projects the team identified, scoped, valued, and prioritized in Steps 3 through 5. These are the opportunities the organization will resource, with people and training, to achieve the goals the Leadership Team developed in Step 2. These opportunities were scoped so they can be accomplished in 90 days.

These ideas/projects, along with the measurement of their implementation status, will be known as Key Performance Indicators (KPIs) in Step 8. The outcome of completing all of the ideas/projects will be the attainment of our "High-Level Business Goals" established in Step 2. KPIs will tell us the status of each idea/project for each month of its implementation journey during the Monthly Business Reviews of Step 10.

Lean Implementation Plan

#	Brainstormed Ideas/Project Descriptions which Support the High-Level Business Goals (Key Performance Indicators)	Lean Tool	R	A	C	I	Status			
1	Reduce Total Cycle Time (from quote to cash) from 67 days to 30 days by the end of Q1	VSM					25%	50%	75%	100%
2	Reduce returns from 3% of sales to less than 1% of sales by the end of Q1	Problem Solving					25%	50%	75%	100%
3	Reduce scrap in the foundry from 6% to 3% of sales by the end of Q1	Problem Solving					25%	50%	75%	100%
4	Reduce set-up time on machine #4 from 3 hours to less than 30 minutes by the end of Q2	Set Up Reduction					25%	50%	75%	100%
5	Reduce finished goods inventory from $9M to less than $3M by the end of Q2	Kanban Kaizen					25%	50%	75%	100%
6	Consolidate warehouses after reducing finished goods inventory by the end of Q3	Project					25%	50%	75%	100%
7	Reduce pricing errors from 9 per order to zero by the end of Q3	Problem Solving					25%	50%	75%	100%
8	Reduce turnover of key personnel from 3% to zero by the end of Q4	Problem Solving					25%	50%	75%	100%
9	Develop a process to respond to an RFQ in a single phone call by the end of Q4	VSM & Process Cell Kaizen					25%	50%	75%	100%
	Additional activities that support the above Kaizen Events & the Lean Culture									
10	Improve hiring / recruiting / training / screening process						25%	50%	75%	100%
11	Conduct Policy Deployment rollout meeting & quarterly updates						25%	50%	75%	100%
12	Provide Lean training for all associates						25%	50%	75%	100%
13	Form Leadership Team office 5S (including training)						25%	50%	75%	100%
14	Clearly define and communicate Behavioral Expectations						25%	50%	75%	100%
15	Develop skills matrix & cross-training plan						25%	50%	75%	100%
16	Cross-train to educate everyone on our Value Streams						25%	50%	75%	100%
17	Implement Visual Management across facility						25%	50%	75%	100%
18	Create a "Sense of Urgency"						25%	50%	75%	100%
19	Create production meeting agenda						25%	50%	75%	100%
20	Create a "Voice of the Customer" program						25%	50%	75%	100%
21	Implement a gain sharing program						25%	50%	75%	100%
22	Develop & implement "New Customer Orientation Program"						25%	50%	75%	100%
23	VSM the Quoting process						25%	50%	75%	100%
24	Implement "Progress Payments" for large jobs						25%	50%	75%	100%
25	Create & implement improved Production Order layout						25%	50%	75%	100%
26	Develop Standard Work Instructions for all processes						25%	50%	75%	100%

Figure #39

Filling In the Lean Implementation Plan Tab

√ Step 7

During the process of listing the identified projects, the team should make recommendations as to which Lean Tool should be used to attack the various opportunities. As illustrated in Figure #39, it was identified that Value Stream Mapping will be used to reduce Total Cycle Time from 67 days to 30 days in Project 1. Structured problem solving should be used to reduce scrap from 6% to 3% in Project 3 and so on down the line.

The next part of the Step 7 process is to add the action items (usually from the Lean Culture or Lean Planning component areas) that need to be implemented first in order to properly support or enable the completion of the ideas/projects that will be worked on by team members. Again, this is where organizations often want to jump to the ideas/projects and start applying the Lean Tools and end up using only 25-35% of Lean's potential as previously shown in Figure #1. To prevent this mistake, a thorough understanding by the team of the four components of Lean is required.

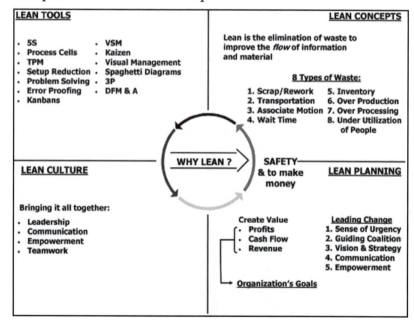

Figure #40
The Four Components of Lean

146

Develop Lean Implementation Plan √

There are two approaches that can be taken at this point to identify support or enabler action items that will be added to the Lean Implementation Plan. The first approach asks questions such as:

- Does the organization have a comprehensive visual and verbal communication plan that touches/reaches all associates on a daily basis?

- Does the organization have the right people in the right jobs or positions?

- Does the Leadership Team need training in leadership development and teamwork?

- Does the organization have the correct structure to support its strategies? Is the company organized around Value Stream and Process Cells or is it still organized by departments?

- Do the middle managers and supervisors completely support Lean and the principle of empowerment?

- Does the organization have a "sense of urgency?"

- Does the organization have a "Guiding Coalition?"

- Do the people within the organization feel empowered to make decisions about their work processes?

- Has everyone in the organization been trained in Lean and teamwork?

147

Step 7

- Does everyone understand the Lean Concepts and the 8 types of waste?

- Has the organization established an organizational-wide "war on waste" culture?

- Does the organization rely on inspection to meet the customers' requirements?

- Has a culture of prevention been established?

- Is the organization customer focused?

- Is the organization committed to safety with a goal of zero?

- Is the organization committed to perfect quality which produces the lowest cost, while doing it right the first time to eliminate all the waste that is associated with doing work over and over again?

- Does the organization understand that Lean applies to transactional processes as well as manufacturing processes?

- Does a Standard Cost Accounting system get in the way of making real improvements?

- Does the organization have meaningful measurements posted in the offices and shop that are aligned to the organizational goals and objectives?

- Does the organization have Standard Work/Job Instructions? Do the people in the organization consistently follow all Standard Work Instructions as part of their Daily Management? Does the organization have and use visual controls in the offices and in the manufacturing areas?

- Are the facilities safe, clean, and organized? Is 5S a part of everyone's daily routine?

This list could go on and on. However, if the answer to any of these questions is "no," then the team must develop an action plan to deal with these various issues. This may take some time, but the team must work through these issues and resolve them in order to create a comprehensive plan that will make Lean a part of the organization's culture.

For most organizations, this means adding enablers such as:

- Lean/Policy Deployment kickoff meetings

- Lean training

- Countermeasures training (Step 9)

- Organization-wide daily measurement systems

- Customer/Supplier meetings

- Communication systems

- Development of a monthly all associates meeting (the World Class standard is a meeting with the top leader in the facility at least monthly)

√ Step 7

The second approach to identifying support or enabler action items is for the team to conduct a "Force Field Analysis." When conducting a Force Field Analysis, the team should take the time to identify all the forces, or things the company is currently doing to work toward its long- term goals and objectives. On the other side of the equation the team would identify all the forces, or things going on in the company that are working against the organization in achieving its business objectives. A Force Field Analysis may look something like Figure #41:

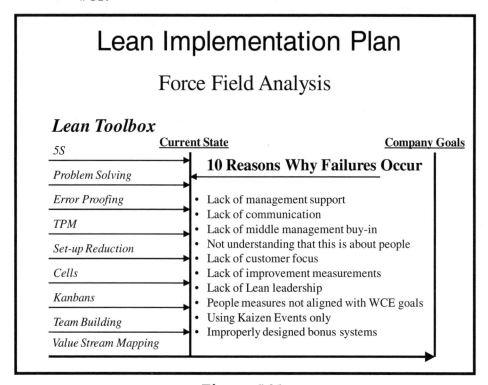

Figure #41
Force Field Analysis

The team then brainstorms action items to add to the Lean Implementation Plan that would enhance the positive things that the organization is currently doing. The team would also identify or brainstorm ideas that would

150

neutralize or mitigate the things that are working against the organization's ability to achieve the business objectives of the organization.

RACI

Once all the improvement opportunities and supporting activities are listed on the project plan (Figure #39), it is time to fill in the RACI (Responsible, Accountable, Consult, & Inform). We start out by identifying the one individual who will be held accountable for each activity.

R Responsible = "The Doers"

A Accountable = "The Buck Stops Here"

C Consult = "Keep in the Loop"

I Inform = "Keep in the Picture"

There can only be one name or set of initials under "Accountable" (Figure #42). You will most likely have more than one set of initials in the "R" column (the people "Responsible" for completing the activity). The "C" represents people we may need to "Consult" with in order to complete the action item. This may include Human Resources, Information Technology, Finance, Legal, some external customer or supplier, or any other individual or group. The "I" stands for those people we need to keep "Informed" while completing the action item. Communication is important in everything an organization does before and during the journey to become World Class. It is extremely important that everyone understand what we are doing and WHY we are doing it!

√ Step 7

Lean Implementation Plan

#	Brainstormed Ideas/Project Descriptions which Support the High-Level Business Goals (Key Performance Indicators)	R	A	C	I	Status
1	Reduce Total Cycle Time (from quote to cash) from 67 days to 30 days by the end of Q1	WCM, ck, pm, dd	LR	WCM	Leadership Team	25% 50% 75% 100%
2	Reduce returns from 3% of sales to less than 1% of sales by the end of Q1	pm, ff, sr, dh	VF	Sales & Marketing	Leadership Team	25% 50% 75% 100%
3	Reduce scrap in the foundry from 6% to 3% of sales by the end of Q1	WCM, dh, sr	MW	Suppliers	Leadership Team	25% 50% 75% 100%
4	Reduce set-up time on machine #4 from 3 hours to less than 30 minutes by the end of Q2	dd, ck, hw	TD	Machine Manufacturers	Leadership Team	25% 50% 75% 100%
5	Reduce finished goods inventory from $9M to less than $3M by the end of Q2	WCM, pm, dh, pb, kl	PL	WCM	Leadership Team	25% 50% 75% 100%
6	Consolidate warehouses after reducing finished goods inventory by the end of Q3	am, ck, ff, pz	PL	Accounting	Leadership Team	25% 50% 75% 100%
7	Reduce pricing errors from 9 per order to zero by the end of Q3	pm, ff, pz, dh	LR	Sales & Marketing	Leadership Team	25% 50% 75% 100%
8	Reduce turnover of key personnel from 3% to zero by the end of Q4	ff, pm, sr	AL	HR	Leadership Team	25% 50% 75% 100%
9	Develop a process to respond to an RFQ in a single phone call by the end of Q4	WCM, am, ck	MW	IT	Leadership Team	25% 50% 75% 100%
	Additional activities that support the above Kaizen Events & the Lean Culture					
10	Improve hiring / recruiting / training / screening process	ck, pm, dd	LR	HR	Leadership Team	25% 50% 75% 100%
11	Conduct Policy Deployment rollout meeting & quarterly updates	pm, ff, sr, dh	VF	kr	Leadership Team	25% 50% 75% 100%
12	Provide Lean training for all associates	WCM, dh, sr	MW	WCM	Leadership Team	25% 50% 75% 100%
13	Form Leadership Team to implement office 5S (including training)	dd, ck, hw	TD	pl	Leadership Team	25% 50% 75% 100%
14	Clearly define and communicate Behavioral Expectations	pm, dh, pb, kl	PL	HR	Leadership Team	25% 50% 75% 100%
15	Develop skills matrix & cross-training plan	am, ck, ff, pz	PL	HR	Leadership Team	25% 50% 75% 100%
16	Cross-train to educate everyone on our Value Streams	pm, ff, pz, dh	LR	HR, td	Leadership Team	25% 50% 75% 100%
17	Implement Visual Management across facility	ff, pm, sr	AL	mw	Leadership Team	25% 50% 75% 100%
18	Create a "Sense of Urgency"	am, ck	MW	Executive staff	Leadership Team	25% 50% 75% 100%
19	Create production meeting agenda	dd, ck, hw	TD	HR	Leadership Team	25% 50% 75% 100%
20	Create a "Voice of the Customer" program	pm, dh, pb, kl	PL	Sales & Marketing	Leadership Team	25% 50% 75% 100%
21	Implement a gain sharing program	am, ck, ff, pz	PL	HR, Legal, WCM	Leadership Team	25% 50% 75% 100%
22	Develop & implement "New Customer Orientation Program"	pm, ff, pz, dh	LR	Sales & Marketing	Leadership Team	25% 50% 75% 100%
23	VSM the Quoting process	ff, pm, sr	AL	WCM	Leadership Team	25% 50% 75% 100%
24	Implement "Progress Payments" for large jobs	am, ck	MW	Sales & Marketing	Leadership Team	25% 50% 75% 100%
25	Create & implement improved Production Order layout	bf, ck, sr	AL	WCM	Leadership Team	25% 50% 75% 100%
26	Develop Standard Work Instructions for all processes	vt, cm, ty	PL	WCM	Leadership Team	25% 50% 75% 100%

Figure #42

The "Status" columns will be filled in during your monthly Lean Implementation Planning meeting covered in Step 10. This is nothing more than shading in the 25%, 50%, 75%, and 100% columns as the action items progress toward completion. The "Accountable" person must monitor the idea/project performance against the plan and immediately take action (see Step 9) if the project turns "red" (project not going as planned). The accountable person must be ready to report the status of the project to the Leadership Team during the Monthly Business Reviews of Step 10.

Before completing the timelines, the team should review how often a particular individual's initials appear in either the "Accountable" or "Responsible" columns. This will determine how aggressive the organization can be in their implementation. If we see the same initials appearing over and over again, we will have to stretch out the timelines. We cannot overextend the available resources in the company. If the team decides that they want to be more aggressive in implementing Lean throughout the organization, they will have to find additional resources to carry out action items on the plan. Remember, the ultimate goal is to involve everyone in the organization in the Deployment activity.

√ Step 7

> ## Team Action for Step 7:
>
> **Load the Excel spreadsheet from the enclosed CD onto your computer. Click on the Tab labeled "Lean Implementation Plan." Have the team insert the project list into the plan. Brainstorm all other support or enabler actions necessary to support these ideas/projects and change the culture in the organization. Complete the RACI and all timelines.**

Develop Lean Implementation Plan √

EXAMPLE

Lean Implementation Plan

#	Brainstormed Ideas/Project Descriptions which Support the High-Level Business Goals (Key Performance Indicators)	Status				Timeline (29-Dec-08 through 20-Apr-09)
1	Reduce Total Cycle Time (from quote to cash) from 67 days to 30 days by the end of Q1	25%	50%	75%	100%	
2	Reduce returns from 3% of sales to less than 1% of sales by the end of Q1	25%	50%	75%	100%	
3	Reduce scrap in the foundry from 6% to 3% of sales by the end of Q1	25%	50%	75%	100%	
4	Reduce set-up time on machine #4 from 3 hours to less than 30 minutes by the end of Q2	25%	50%	75%	100%	
5	Reduce finished goods inventory from $9M to less than $3M by the end of Q2	25%	50%	75%	100%	
6	Consolidate warehouses after reducing finished goods inventory by the end of Q3	25%	50%	75%	100%	
7	Reduce pricing errors from 9 per order to zero by the end of Q3	25%	50%	75%	100%	
8	Reduce turnover of key personnel from 3% to zero by the end of Q4	25%	50%	75%	100%	
9	Develop a process to respond to an RFQ in a single phone call by the end of Q4	25%	50%	75%	100%	
	Additional activities that support the above Kaizen Events & the Lean Culture					
10	Improve hiring / recruiting / training / screening process	25%	50%	75%	100%	
11	Conduct Policy Deployment rollout meeting & quarterly updates	25%	50%	75%	100%	
12	Provide Lean training for all associates	25%	50%	75%	100%	
13	Form Leadership Team to implement office 5S (including training)	25%	50%	75%	100%	
14	Clearly define and communicate Behavioral Expectations	25%	50%	75%	100%	
15	Develop skills matrix & cross-training plan	25%	50%	75%	100%	

Legend:
- ■ = Project Start/End Date
- │ = Project Timeline
- ▦ = "RED" Project (Script B) Requires Countermeasure

155

Step 8:

Develop Bowling Chart

STEP 8 OBJECTIVE

Develop a monthly measurement chart (twelve-frame bowling chart) to track how the Lean activities from Step 7 are impacting the organization's goals established in Step 2. This chart will be the subject of the Monthly Business Review meetings of Step 10.

√ **Step 8**

10 Steps to Successful Policy Deployment

1. Establish a Mission and Guiding Principles

2. Develop Business Goals

3. Brainstorm for Opportunities to Achieve Goals

4. Define Parameters to Value Opportunities

5. Establish Weighting Requirements, Rate Opportunities, and Prioritize

6. Conduct a Reality Check

7. Develop Lean Implementation Plan

8. **Develop Bowling Chart**

9. Countermeasures

10. Conducting Business Reviews

At this point the team knows the company goals, and has identified, scoped, valued, and prioritized key projects to achieve the goals. They have developed the Lean Implementation Plan and understand the timing of the projects, and more importantly, when the projects will start to show results. The Lean Implementation Plan (Step 7) has listed all the key projects that must be completed to achieve the business objectives of the organization and all the supporting or enabler activities necessary to support the projects and required culture change. Now, before the team can resource, train, and launch high impact sub-teams that are empowered to achieve the goals, a scoreboard must be developed.

The scoreboard is referred to as a "Bowling Chart (Figure #43). There are twelve months in a financial year and twelve frames in the game of bowling. The Bowling Chart will give the Leadership Team the ability to monitor progress toward the goals on a monthly basis and, as will be shown, the people responsible for each metric will need to monitor progress on a daily basis. In this way the team will be able to hold each other responsible and accountable for getting the results.

The first thing that must be done on the Bowling Chart is to change, if necessary, the twelve months at the top of the spreadsheet to correspond with the months in your organization's fiscal year. Many organizations have their fiscal year correspond to the calendar year; however, there are organizations that have their fiscal year begin in October.

Now layer in the high-level Business Goals that were identified in Step 2 under the column labeled "High Level Business Goals." Generally these goals are highlighted because they are the results of the projects that

Develop Bowling Chart √

#	High-Level Business Goals & Key Performance Indicators (KPIs)	Owner	JOP	YTD		Jan	Feb	Mar
	High-Level Business Goals							
1	Achieve ZERO lost injury days for the next 12 months	MW	5	0	Plan	0	0	0
				0	Act	0	0	0
2	Improve Net Income from 3% to 8% of sales by the end of the fiscal year	LR	3.0%	3.0%	Plan	3.0%	3.0%	3.0%
				2.8%	Act	3.0%	3.2%	2.2%
3	Improve Free Cash Flow from 30% of net income to 70% of net income by the end of the fiscal year	VF	30.0%	30%	Plan	30%	30%	30%
				34%	Act	31%	34%	37%
4	Increase Revenue from $32 million to $36 million without eroding profits by the end of the fiscal year	LR	$32 M	$7.8	Plan	$2.6	$2.6	$2.6
				$8.1	Act	$2.6	$2.7	$2.8
	Key Performance Indicators (KPIs)							
5	Reduce System Cycle Time (from quote to cash) from 67 days to 30 days by the end of Q1	LR	67 days	54 days	Plan	67 days	50 days	45 days
				51 days	Act	67 days	47 days	40 days
6	Reduce returns from 3% of sales to less than 1% of sales by the end of Q1	VF	3.0%	3.0%	Plan	3.0%	3.0%	3.0%
				3.4%	Act	3.2%	3.0%	4.0%
7	Reduce scrap in the foundry from 6% to 3% of sales by the end of Q1	MW	6.0%	6.0%	Plan	6.0%	6.0%	6.0%
				5.8%	Act	5.8%	5.6%	6.0%

Bowling Chart 1: Insert the correct months that represent the company's fiscal year

Bowling Chart 2: Insert the organizational goals established in Step 2

Bowling Chart 3: Convert, if necessary, the brainstormed ideas/project goals to SMART goals and consolidate wherever possible. Example: If the team has a couple of projects that deal with reducing setup times and several projects that deal with improving up-time on machines, the team may decide to cluster all of these improvement initiatives into one OEE metric.

☐ = Project is at or above goal (Script A)
▨ = Project is "RED" (below goal) and requires a countermeasure (Script B)

Figure #43

√ *Step 8*

will be implemented as part of our Lean Implementation plan (Step 7). Underneath the "High-Level Business Goals" we will list our KPI's or Key Performance Indicators. There may be a KPI for each project that is listed in our Lean Implementation plan or several projects could be combined into one KPI. For example, if we decide to have one project that will reduce setup time on one printing press (using the setup reduction tool to reduce the change-over/make ready time from 4 hours to 2 hours) and another project that focuses on a printing press that experiences frequent breakdowns (using total productive maintenance (TPM) to improve the uptime on this press by 50%), we may be able to combine these metrics into one overall OEE metric. This decision is entirely up to the team and is based on how much stratification is required to run the business and hold people accountable and responsible.

Now that a time frame for each improvement initiative has been established (established in Steps 6 and 7), we can establish a "SMART" goal for each improvement project that has been identified. This is the goal that the Leadership Team will use to kickoff each Kaizen Event. These SMART goals are generally expressed in the form of operational metrics to which people can relate.

Most people in organizations do not understand many of the financial terms or ratios such as operating income, EBITDA, ROIC, inventory turns, and free cash flow. However, most people understand operational metrics and can help the organization improve them. They can associate with reducing scrap from 6% to 3% by the end of the third quarter or reducing the change-over time on machine #4 from 3 hours 20 minutes to 1 hour 10 minutes.

160

Develop Bowling Chart √

#	High-Level Business Goals & Key Performance Indicators (KPIs)	Owner	JOP		YTD		Jan	Feb	Mar
	High-Level Business Goals								
1	Achieve ZERO lost injury days for the next 12 months	MW	5	Plan	0		0	0	0
				Act	0		0	0	0
2	Improve Net Income from 3% to 8% of sales by the end of the fiscal year	LR	3.0%	Plan	3.0%		3.0%	3.0%	3.0%
				Act	2.8%		3.0%	3.2%	2.2%
3	Improve Free Cash Flow from 30% of net income to 70% of net income by the end of the fiscal year	VF	30.0%	Plan	30%		30%	30%	30%
				Act	34%		31%	34%	37%
4	Increase Revenue from $32 million to $36 million without eroding profits by the end of the fiscal year	LR	$32 M	Plan	$7.8		$2.6	$2.6	$2.6
				Act	$8.1		$2.6	$2.7	$2.8
	Key Performance Indicators (KPIs)								
5	Reduce System Cycle Time (from quote to cash) from 67 days to 30 days by the end of Q1	LR	67 days	Plan	54 days		67 days	50 days	45 days
				Act	51 days		67 days	47 days	40 days
6	Reduce returns from 3% of sales to less than 1% of sales by the end of Q1	VF	3.0%	Plan	3.0%		3.0%	3.0%	3.0%
				Act	3.4%		3.2%	3.0%	4.0%
7	Reduce scrap in the foundry from 6% to 3% of sales by the end of Q1	MW	6.0%	Plan	6.0%		6.0%	6.0%	6.0%
				Act	5.8%		5.8%	5.6%	6.0%

Bowling Chart 5: Enter "Jumping Off Point." "Where are you today?

Bowling Chart 4: Establish an owner for each metric. Only one name can appear here. This is the person who will have to do a "Countermeasure" if the metric turns "Red".

☐ = Project is at or above goal (Script A)
■ = Project is "RED" (below goal) and requires a countermeasure (Script B)

Figure #44

√ Step 8

PROBLEMS ARE SOLVABLE EXCUSES ARE FOREVER

Every KPI must have an owner. Under the column marked "Owner" put the initials of the individual who will be held accountable for that KPI during the monthly Business Review meetings of Step 10 (Figure #44). This is the person who should be meeting with his/her team on a daily basis and reviewing their metrics which are displayed on charts and graphs in the area where the Kaizen Event or improvement activity took place. This is part of what is referred to as "Daily Management" which is also covered in Step 2. It will also be this owner's responsibility to work with his/her team to develop immediate "countermeasures" (discussed in Step 9) if they see the KPI trending below their SMART goal. The owner and the team must be empowered to take immediate countermeasure action to put them back on target of achieving their SMART goal.

In addition to establishing the owner of each metric, the Leadership Team will establish the JOP or "Jumping Off Point" for each metric. So if the goal is to improve our OEE metric to 71%, we need to know what it is today—what is our starting point.

The next part of Step 8 is to take the information or project timing that we developed during the Lean Implementation Planning process and make a determination on when we can expect to see the results hitting our KPI's or the bottom line of our business (Figure #45). These are the numbers we insert in the row labeled "Plan" for each KPI. These numbers are month to month forecasted improvement numbers as a result of the Kaizen Events. They are not cumulative numbers. Under the column labeled "YTD" (Year To Date) we insert the cumulative numbers for both the KPI and actuals for the year or accumulated results.

Develop Bowling Chart √

#	High-Level Business Goals & Key Performance Indicators (KPIs)	Owner	JOP	YTD		Jan	Feb	Mar
	High-Level Business Goals							
1	Achieve ZERO lost injury days for the next 12 months	MW	5	0	Plan	0	0	0
				0	Act	0	0	0
2	Improve Net Income from 3% to 8% of sales by the end of the fiscal year	LR	3.0%	3.0%	Plan	3.0%	3.0%	3.0%
				2.8%	Act	3.0%	3.2%	2.2%
3	Improve Free Cash Flow from 30% of net income to 70% of net income by the end of the fiscal year	VF	30.0%	30%	Plan	30%	30%	30%
				34%	Act	31%	34%	37%
4	Increase Revenue from $32 million to $36 million without eroding profits by the end of the fiscal year	LR	$32 M	$7.8	Plan	$2.6	$2.6	$2.6
				$8.1	Act	$2.6	$2.7	$2.8
	Key Performance Indicators (KPIs)							
5	Reduce System Cycle Time (from quote to cash) from 67 days to 30 days by the end of Q1	LR	67 days	54 days	Plan	67 days	50 days	45 days
				51 days	Act	67 days	47 days	40 days
6	Reduce returns from 3% of sales to less than 1% of sales by the end of Q1	VF	3.0%	3.0%	Plan	3.0%	3.0%	3.0%
				3.4%	Act	3.0%	3.0%	4.0%
7	Reduce scrap in the foundry from 6% to 3% of sales by the end of Q1	MW	6.0%	6.0%	Plan	6.0%	6.0%	6.0%
				5.8%	Act		5.6%	

Bowling Chart 6: From Step 7 "Lean Implementation Plan" the team now knows which projects they will run and when. Enter the "Plan" numbers under the appropriate month. These are the numbers we **must** meet to achieve the business goals.

☐ = Project is at or above goal (Script A)
▓ = Project is "RED" (below goal) and requires a countermeasure (Script B)

Figure #45

√ *Step 8*

The "Plan" line can also show the difference between "Daily Management" and "Breakthrough Goals." We were working with a company recently to determine what numbers should be put in their plan to reflect a reduction in product quality issues. During the development of the "Impact Analysis Worksheet," we discovered that, for the last fiscal year, their quality issues cost the company $600,000 annually, with a monthly average around $50,000.

We then asked the individual in charge of this metric, "How much could we reduce this monthly number if we systematically attacked this using structured problem solving (DMAIC)?" After some discussion this person concluded that we could indeed chip away at this company-wide problem and get approximately $5,000 of savings every month. Consequently, we entered $45,000 per month under the plan line until we launched a more formal Kaizen event later in the year. Once the Kaizen event was completed we expected to see this monthly number drop to $25,000 per month.

Our "Bowling Chart" is now ready to be populated by the monthly "actual" numbers for each KPI (Figure #46). Again, any monthly or year-to-date numbers that turn "Red" must have a countermeasure as outlined in the next chapter.

This is where the rubber meets the road. Organizations that fail do so because of poor execution. The excuses are numerous: we do not have the time to implement our plan, too many fires to fight, we do not have enough good people, or we do not have the resources to make this happen. These are the same organizations that lack good Daily Management.

Develop Bowling Chart √

#	High-Level Business Goals & Key Performance Indicators (KPIs)	Owner	JOP	YTD		Jan	Feb	Mar
	High-Level Business Goals							
1	Achieve ZERO lost injury days for the next 12 months	MW	5	0	Plan	0	0	0
				0	Act	0	0	0
2	Improve Net Income from 3% to 8% of sales by the end of the fiscal year	LR	3.0%	3.0%	Plan	3.0%	3.0%	3.0%
				2.8%	Act	3.0%	3.2%	2.2%
3	Improve Free Cash Flow from 30% of net income to 70% of net income by the end of the fiscal year	VF	30.0%	30%	Plan	30%	30%	30%
				34%	Act	31%	34%	37%
4	Increase Revenue from $32 million to $36 million without eroding profits by the end of the fiscal year	LR	$32 M	$7.8	Plan	$2.6	$2.6	$2.6
				$8.1	Act	$2.6	$2.7	$2.8
	Key Performance Indicators (KPIs)							
5	Reduce System Cycle Time (from quote to cash) from 67 days to 30 days by the end of Q1	LR	67 days	54 days	Plan	67 days	50 days	45 days
				51 days	Act	67 days	47 days	40 days
6	Reduce returns from 3% of sales to less than 1% of sales by the end of Q1	VF	3.0%	3.0%	Plan	3.0%	3.0%	3.0%
				3.4%	Act	3.0%	3.0%	4.0%
7	Reduce scrap in the foundry from 6% to 3% of sales by the end of Q1	MW	6.0%	6.0%	Plan	6.0%	6.0%	6.0%
				5.8%	Act	6%	6%	6.0%

Bowling Chart Z: Enter the "Actual" and "Year to Date" numbers on a monthly basis. The owner of each number should not wait until the end of the month to find out whether or not the team hit their goal. The team needs to develop daily operational metrics to be able to take the appropriate corrective action. Any number that turns "RED" must have a countermeasure.

▢ = Project is at or above goal (Script A)
▣ = Project is "RED" (below goal) and requires a countermeasure (Script B)

Figure #46

√ **Step 8**

Good leaders do not make excuses for not getting things done. They make things happen. Leaders create a vision of where the organization will be in one, three, and five years down the road. They put a plan in place to make the vision a reality. They communicate the vision and the plan over and over again. Then they empower their people to make it happen. The people will help you, if you let them. They will need training and guidance, but that is what good leadership is all about.

TEAM ACTION FOR STEP 8:

Load the Excel spreadsheet from the enclosed CD onto your computer. Click on the tab labeled "Bowling Chart." Complete the Bowling Chart as follows:

1. **Insert the months that properly represent the organization's fiscal year**

2. **Enter the organizational goals established in Step 2**

3. **Take all project goals and, if necessary, restate them as "from ___ to ___" and ensure they are SMART goals**

4. **Establish an owner for each metric**

5. **Enter the current metric or "Jumping Off Point"**

6. **Based on the time lines established in Step 6, layer in the monthly targets for each operational metric**

7. **Enter monthly "Actual" as they are collected. Any number that turns "RED" must have a countermeasure**

Develop Bowling Chart √

EXAMPLE

#	High-Level Business Goals & Key Performance Indicators (KPIs)	Owner	JOP	YTD		Jan	Feb	Mar
	High-Level Business Goals							
1	Achieve ZERO lost injury days for the next 12 months	MW	5	0	Plan	0	0	0
				0	Act	0	0	0
2	Improve Net Income from 3% to 8% of sales by the end of the fiscal year	LR	3.0%	3.0%	Plan	3.0%	3.0%	3.0%
				2.8%	Act	3.0%	3.2%	2.2%
3	Improve Free Cash Flow from 30% of net income to 70% of net income by the end of the fiscal year	VF	30.0%	30%	Plan	30%	30%	30%
				34%	Act	31%	34%	37%
4	Increase Revenue from $32 million to $36 million without eroding profits by the end of the fiscal year	LR	$32 M	$7.8	Plan	$2.6	$2.6	$2.6
				$8.1	Act	$2.6	$2.7	$2.8
	Key Performance Indicators (KPIs)							
5	Reduce System Cycle Time (from quote to cash) from 67 days to 30 days by the end of Q1	LR	67 days	54 days	Plan	67 days	50 days	45 days
				51 days	Act	67 days	47 days	40 days
6	Reduce returns from 3% of sales to less than 1% of sales by the end of Q1	VF	3.0%	3.0%	Plan	3.0%	3.0%	3.0%
				3.4%	Act	3.2%	3.0%	4.0%
7	Reduce scrap in the foundry from 6% to 3% of sales by the end of Q1	MW	6.0%	6.0%	Plan	6.0%	6.0%	6.0%
				5.8%	Act	5.8%	5.6%	6.0%
8	Reduce set-up time on machine #4 from 3 hours to less than 30 minutes by the end of Q2	TD	180 min	180	Plan	180	180	180
				180	Act	180	170	190
9	Reduce finished goods inventory from $9 million to less than $3 million by the end of Q2	PL	$9M	$8.67	Plan	$9.00	$9.00	$8.00
				$8.50	Act	$9.00	$8.50	$8.00
10	Consolidate warehouses after reducing finished goods inventory by the end of Q3 -- potential cost saving of $800K	PL	Project	$0.0	Plan	$0.0	$0.0	$0.0
				$0.0	Act	$0.0	$0.0	$0.0
11	Reduce pricing errors from 9 per order to zero by the end of Q3	LR	9	9	Plan	9	9	9
				7	Act	9	7	5
12	Reduce turnover of key personnel from 3% to zero by the end of Q4	AL	3.0%	3.0%	Plan	3.0%	3.0%	3.0%
				2.1%	Act	3.6%	0.0%	2.8%
13	Develop a process to respond to an RFQ in a single phone call by the end of Q4	MW	3 Days	3 Days	Plan	3 Days	3 Days	3 Days
				3 Days	Act	3 Days	3 Days	3 Days

▭ = Project is at or above goal (Script A)
▬ = Project is "RED" (below goal) and requires a countermeasure (Script B)

167

Step 9:

Countermeasures

STEP 9 OBJECTIVE

Implement countermeasures, which are the Lean and Six Sigma tools that allow the team(s) to make adjustments in their implementation plan (Step 7) if they discover from their daily measurement system that they are below target. Countermeasure tools include:

- Team Problem Solving
- Error Proofing
- DMAIC

√ **Step 9**

10 Steps to Successful Policy Deployment

1. Establish a Mission and Guiding Principles

2. Develop Business Goals

3. Brainstorm for Opportunities to Achieve Goals

4. Define Parameters to Value Opportunities

5. Establish Weighting Requirements, Rate Opportunities, and Prioritize

6. Conduct a Reality Check

7. Develop Lean Implementation Plan

8. Develop Bowling Chart

9. **Countermeasures**

10. Conducting Business Reviews

One of the greatest accomplishments in American history is the landing of Apollo 11 on the lunar surface. Not many people will forget the famous words uttered by Neil Armstrong, "That's one small step for man, one giant leap for mankind."

Just as amazing, and maybe even more heroic, was the dramatic rescue effort of the crew of Apollo 13. Most people have heard the quote, "Houston, we have a problem." The quote was made by Jim Lovell (played by Tom Hanks in the film Apollo 13). As impactful as that quote was, there was an even more significant quote made by the Flight Director Gene Kranz (played by Ed Harris) as they were planning how to get the Apollo 13 crew home safely, "We've never lost an American in space and we're sure as hell not gonna lose one on my watch! Failure is not an option!"

Does your company have the same attitude about achieving its commitments to the goals and objectives of the organization? After all, we are talking about the future of the company, and people's jobs and livelihoods. Does your organization have the same sense of urgency that Flight Director Gene Kranz had during Apollo 13, no matter how aggressive the target? Does your organization have an attitude that reflects the principle that, "Failure is not an option!"?

In this Policy Deployment process, the team established goals for the organization, defined how we expect the organization to behave in achieving the goals, put an action plan in place to achieve the goals, and established the Bowling Chart to track progress. The Leadership team cannot now accept failure. Remember, "Failure is not an option!" Even though the team may have established break-through or stretch goals for the organization which may seem unattainable, they must insist on driving for the expected results. The Leadership Team must help each other and hold each other accountable to achieve the desired outcomes.

The Leadership Team cannot become complacent. Even though we may be making great progress toward the organization's goals, the Leadership team MUST NOT accept anything less than goal. Anything on the Bowling Chart that turns RED is an out-of-control condition and must be dealt with using structured problem solving.

KPI owners do not come to a Monthly Business Review meeting (Step 10) with problems. They come to the meeting with solutions. This means that, for all goals, action items, and metrics for which they are responsible, they must have a way of monitoring progress on a daily basis. If their daily metrics show that things are not going according to plan, they must meet with their team to put a plan in place that will allow the organization to get back on track. The team must meet and progress through a structured problem solving methodology.

The most common structured problem solving methodology in use today comes out of the Six Sigma process. The Six Sigma structured problem solving process is generally referred to as the DMAIC [duh-may-ick] process (Define, Measure, Analyze, Improve, and Control).

- Define: What is the problem?

- Measure: How bad is the problem?

- Analyze: What are the causes?

- Improve: What action do we need to take?

√ Step 9

♦ Control: How do we sustain our improvements?

Following this structured problem solving process will encourage and stimulate creative thinking and lead a team through a series of logical steps, from defining a problem to implementing solutions linked to underlying causes, and establishing best practices to ensure the solutions stay in place.

Within the define, measure, analyze, improve, and control structured problem solving process, there are steps that will effectively guide the decisions of the process owner and the team (See Figure #47):

DEFINE	MEASURE	ANALYZE	IMPROVE	CONTROL
Define customer, process, and supplier requirements	Conduct a requirements review using a SIPOC	Identify gaps between current performance & goal performance	Develop potential solutions	Brainstorm & implement Error Proofing as required
Define the problem (clear problem statement), set goal, & define project scope/set boundaries	Create a process map paying close attention to critical quality characteristics & non-value added time	Identify sources of variation	Evaluate, select & optimize best solutions	Develop & implement Standard Work Instructions, training plan, visual communications, & process controls
Map or flow chart the process	Identify key input, process, & output metrics	Identify the "vital few" key process input variables that affect key outputs..."find the control knobs"	Develop & implement pilot solution	Implement solutions & on-going process measurements
Identify project team & support people	Develop data collection plan	Prioritize opportunities for improvement	Confirm attainment of project goals	Identify opportunities to apply project lessons
Create communication plan	Validate measurement system	Estimate impact of root causes on key outputs	Develop full-scale implementation plan	Complete "Control" Gate Review
Complete "Define" Gate Review	Collect baseline data	Complete "Analyze" Gate Review	Complete "Improve" Gate Review	Transition monitoring/control to process owner
	Determine process capability			
	Complete "Measure" Gate Review			

Figure #47

172

It is important to follow this basic structure. What tends to happen in most organizations is that management believes they know what all the issues are and they tend to jump to the solution. They may be right, but then again, they may be wrong. They also do not create an environment to explore creative solutions. The following are nine pitfalls to creative problem solving:

1. The problem is too large, too general, or not well-defined

2. Failing to involve employees affected by the problem or critical decision makers during solution identification

3. Rush to judgment before completely analyzing the problem

4. Attacking problems beyond the control of the team

5. Failing to seek creative solutions and following hidden agendas

6. Assassinating creative ideas before exploring their full potential

7. Choosing a solution for the wrong reasons

8. Failing to plan for the implementation of the chosen solution

9. Failing to follow-up on the solution's effectiveness

√ Step 9

The charter of this book is not intended to be a complete study of structured problem solving. There are many books out there that would present a more comprehensive approach to the subject. It may also be necessary to have Six Sigma Black Belts or other dedicated, trained personnel that can help the team better understand structured problem solving. The important thing is that the organization understands that they cannot accept deviations from the goals or failure.

It is important that the organization develops a driving determination to achieve the goals and objectives they have set for themselves. It is just as important that management does not get in the way of the people who can really resolve problems or improve processes. It has been our experience that when some companies start to fail in achieving their goals and objectives, the company starts to micro-manage the business. This is the last thing that should happen. Management thinks they know what all the issues are or have all the answers, so they start to implement their solutions. This tends to make matters worse and then it is a downward spiraling situation.

Identify who is accountable or the owner for each item on the Lean Implementation Plan (Step 7) and each Key Performance Indicators (KPI's) on the Bowling Chart (Step 8). When either of these two steps are not meeting expectations (turns RED), have the responsible individual work with his/her team to systematically get back on track. Use structured problem solving to get back on track—the simpler the tools and the quicker the response the better.

When using structured problem solving, do not get stuck in "analysis paralysis." Some organizations think that they need to get together in a large team and study the problem to death. World Class enterprises use structured problem solving as a way of life. They would simply conduct a stand up meeting and define the problem in simple terms (DEFINE). Because they are World Class, they have metrics in place that indicate there is a problem in the first place (MEASURE). They may use a Fish Bone Diagram to identify all potential root causes, 3-2-1 voting to establish the top issues, and a technique known as the 5 Why's to get to the root cause(s) (ANALYZE). They would then brainstorm all potential solutions, affinitize (cluster like ideas together) the list, multi-vote to establish the best solutions, and then develop an implementation plan (who is going to do what by when) (IMPROVE). Once they have tested and verified that their solution has the organization back on track they would then make everyone involved aware of the process changes, educate the people as required, identify and implement error-proofing devices, establish standard work instructions and visual controls, and monitor the process to ensure conformity (CONTROL).

Remember, the simpler the tools the better—speed is a competitive advantage.

Define

There are simple, useful tools that can be used in each of the DMAIC process steps. Probably the most important tool or step in the "define" stage is ensuring that the team has properly defined the problem.

The problem statement must be a clear, simple statement of what is not happening the way it is supposed to be happening. The problem statement should not identify the cause of the problem, nor should the problem statement suggest what corrective action should be taken. Problem statements should take the following format:

√ Step 9

1. Customer returns are running $50,000 over budget

2. Scrap & rework are exceeding our goal by 3%

3. 50% of the orders entered into our systems have errors on them

There are times when the team may have to use a tool known as a SIPOC to better understand the work process, or what is the problem, or what requirements are not being met. SIPOC stand for Supplier, Inputs, Process, Outputs, and Customer.

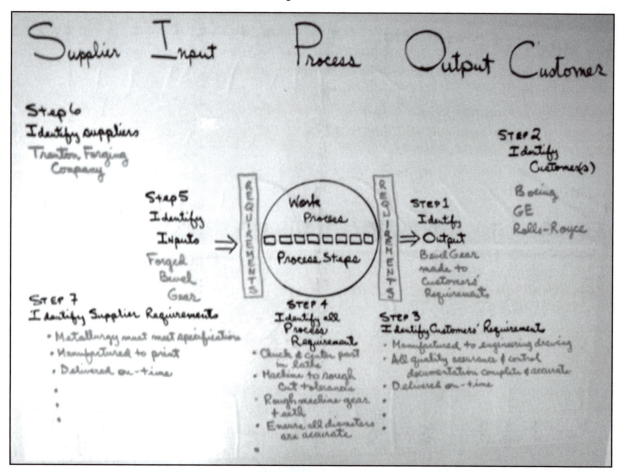

Figure #48
SIPOC Chart

Creating a SIPOC is accomplished in seven parts or steps (see Figure #48).

1. Identify Outputs—understand the process that is used to produce the output. This could be a physical product or an information product.

2. Identify Customer(s)—who are the customer(s) of the process?

3. Identify the Customer's Requirements.

4. Identify all Process Requirements—all process requirements must be thoroughly reviewed and understood by everyone. All value-added work is a process—a step-by-step sequence of events that results in the production of a physical product or information product.

5. Identify Inputs—identify all the inputs coming into the process.

6. Identify Suppliers—determine who supplies these inputs.

7. Identify Supplier Requirements—what are the requirements of those items coming into the process?

A requirement review is then used to ensure we understand the customer requirements, process requirements, and supplier requirements. At this stage, we are trying to understand the current process. The team may start to identify all kinds of issues or misunderstandings that are causing the problem. Do not jump ahead. During the Analyze step, we will start to determine what needs

Step 9

to change in this process to prevent recurring problems or defects. Remember, when we talk about structured problem solving, we are talking about procedural changes. We do not have people problems, we have process problems.

Measure

What should we be measuring? We should be measuring non-conformances. A non-conformance is a requirement that is not met. If your company has not established and communicated customer requirements, process requirements, and supplier requirements, you cannot have a non-conformance. This tends to be a shock for most companies because they do not take the time to conduct a thorough requirements review for all key, core, and critical processes. Nor do they take the time to ensure that everyone knows, understands, and follows processes consistently. Have you ever been in a situation where people on one shift do things differently than people on a different shift?

Once we take the time to establish customer, process, and supplier requirements, we must take these requirements seriously. Management must lead by example. If management walks around and says things like, "that's close enough," then no one will take requirements seriously. The company then begins to lack the necessary DISCIPLINE to manage variation in their processes. It is essential to establish a company culture where all requirements are known, understood, and taken seriously.

Countermeasures √

Analyze

The best tool to begin analyzing a problem is the Cause and Effect Diagram, sometimes known as a Fishbone Diagram or an Ishikawa Diagram. As illustrated in Figure #49, we begin by putting the "effect" or desired result in the box at the tip of the arrow. In the example below the issue was over and under size diameters. The team would then brainstorm all potential "causes." This brainstorming activity is done in a structured environment. When brainstorming, try to place items under one of six categories: People, Assessment, Material, Environment, Equipment, and Methods (See also Figure #50).

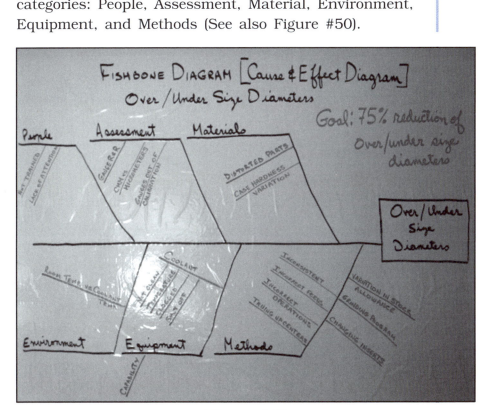

**Figure #49
Fishbone Diagram**

Anything that could cause a diameter to be over or under size during a machining operation is noted.

√ *Step 9*

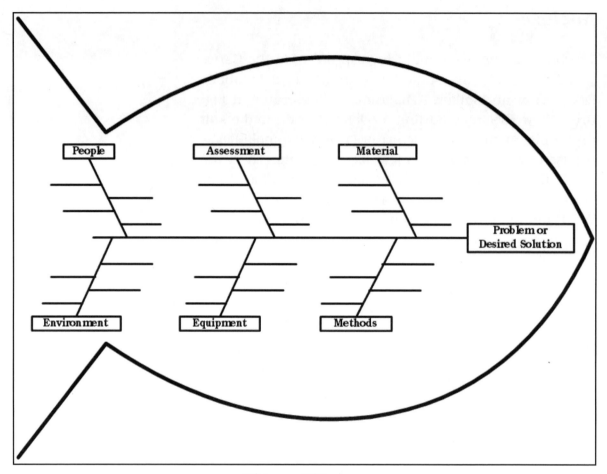

**Figure #50
Fishbone Diagram**

Do not get hung up on whether something belongs under one category or the other. Use the rules for brainstorming and capture everyone's ideas. Once all the ideas have been captured, it is time to conduct some investigations. Obviously, there are many more statistical tools that could be used at this time, but it is amazing how well the people know the process and all the potential causes.

After the team has had the opportunity to discuss and possibly investigate the causes presented, it is time to do 3-2-1 voting. Everyone places a "3" next to the item that they think is the biggest contributor to the problem or desired solution; they put a "2" next to the next biggest contributor, and a "1" next to their third and final choice. All numbers are then added up and the causes that have the greatest number would be at the top of the list, and so on down the list.

The team will now conduct an exercise known as the 5 Whys (see Figure #51). For each of the top items, the facilitator would ask a team member "why" at least five times to get to the "root" cause of the problem/question. For example, if the team has identified that coolant is the number one culprit for over/under size diameters and the facilitator ask, "why is coolant causing over/under size diameters?" The response might be that there is temperature variation causing the metal to expand and contract during the final grinding operation. When asked, "Why is there temperature variation?" the response might be that the coolant tanks are too close to the exterior wall and during the winter time the coolant gets extremely cold. The facilitator would continue to ask these kinds of questions, trying to get the team to dig deeper and deeper into all the issues. The team continues to explore all potential root causes. This exercise tends to drive people crazy after awhile, but it really gets people to think.

Once all the potential root causes have been explored it is time to move into the next phase of structured problem solving.

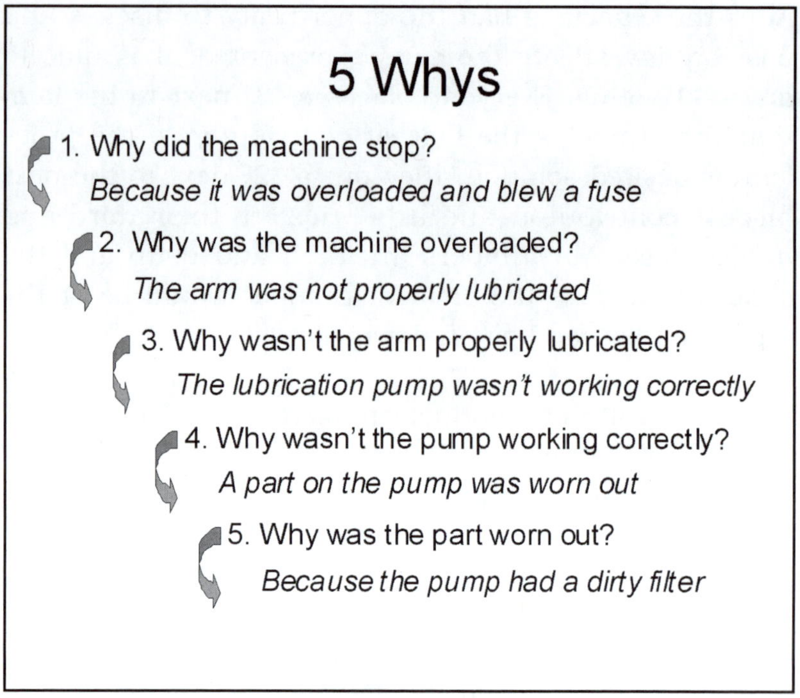

√ *Step 9*

> # 5 Whys
>
> 1. Why did the machine stop?
>   *Because it was overloaded and blew a fuse*
> 2. Why was the machine overloaded?
>   *The arm was not properly lubricated*
> 3. Why wasn't the arm properly lubricated?
>   *The lubrication pump wasn't working correctly*
> 4. Why wasn't the pump working correctly?
>   *A part on the pump was worn out*
> 5. Why was the part worn out?
>   *Because the pump had a dirty filter*

**Figure #51
5 Whys Example**

Note that in the example shown in Figure #51, a 6th Why, "Why did the pump have a dirty filter?", and possibly a 7th Why could be asked. Experience shows that 75% of the time 5 Whys will expose the root cause but there will be problems where it will only take 4 Whys and other problems that will require 6 Whys or more.

Improve

For each root cause, the team should use brainstorming to identify all potential solutions. Brainstorming is a critical step to the "improve" process. A trained facilitator is required for this process, to ensure that the team truly understands the rules for effective brainstorming, so they can really identify all potential solutions. The rules for brainstorming are:

√ *State problem in the form of a question*

   Whenever possible state the idea in the form of a question. How can we reduce finished goods inventory from $2.0M to less than $750K? How can we reduce order entry from 3 days to 1 hour? How can we reduce the time it takes to admit a patient in emergency from 3 hours to less than 10 minutes?

√ *Record all ideas on a flip chart and number them*

   Have a skilled facilitator record all ideas on a flip chart and hang them around the room. Do not get hung up on spelling things correctly—it is a very narrow mind that can spell something only one way. Use many different colors; it stimulates the creative thought process.

√ *Quantity of ideas most important*

   It is not uncommon to generate a hundred or more ideas. Do not be concerned if there is a lull in the generation of ideas, just wait, the ideas will come. Maybe take a break, get some fresh air, then start the process up again.

√ *Step 9*

√ *No criticism, discussion, or judgment is allowed until all ideas have been presented. Clarification questions are okay.*

This is a tough one, and really requires a skilled facilitator. No one is to criticize someone else's idea —verbally or non-verbally. It is okay to ask clarifying questions so that the scope of the idea is understood, but do not analyze ideas at this time.

√ *Encourage participation by all*

We encourage participation by all by going around the room, in order, so everyone gets a chance to put an idea on the flip chart. This prevents the more outspoken people in the room from dominating the meeting and allows the more reserved individuals to participate. Only one idea can be given per turn and if a person does not have an idea when it is his or her turn that person just says "pass."

√ *Piggyback—build on each other's ideas*

It is desirable to piggyback your idea off of someone else's, but you have to wait your turn.

√ *Don't limit thinking or imagination—thinking "outside the box" is required here!*

It is easier to tame down a wild idea than to build up a bland idea. Let your imaginations run wild.

√ *When all ideas have been presented, review each for feasibility and impact*

After consolidating like ideas and discussing the feasibility of each, the team can use a tool known as multi-voting to narrow the list down to a manageable size. In multi-voting each team member has a set number of votes to use to vote for the ideas they think will have the greatest impact on resolving the problem or reaching the desired outcome.

The voting is done by secret ballot so as not to influence other people's opinions. The solutions with the greatest number of votes are the ideas the team will implement. These ideas then formulate the basis for the Kaizen Newspaper (See Figure #52).

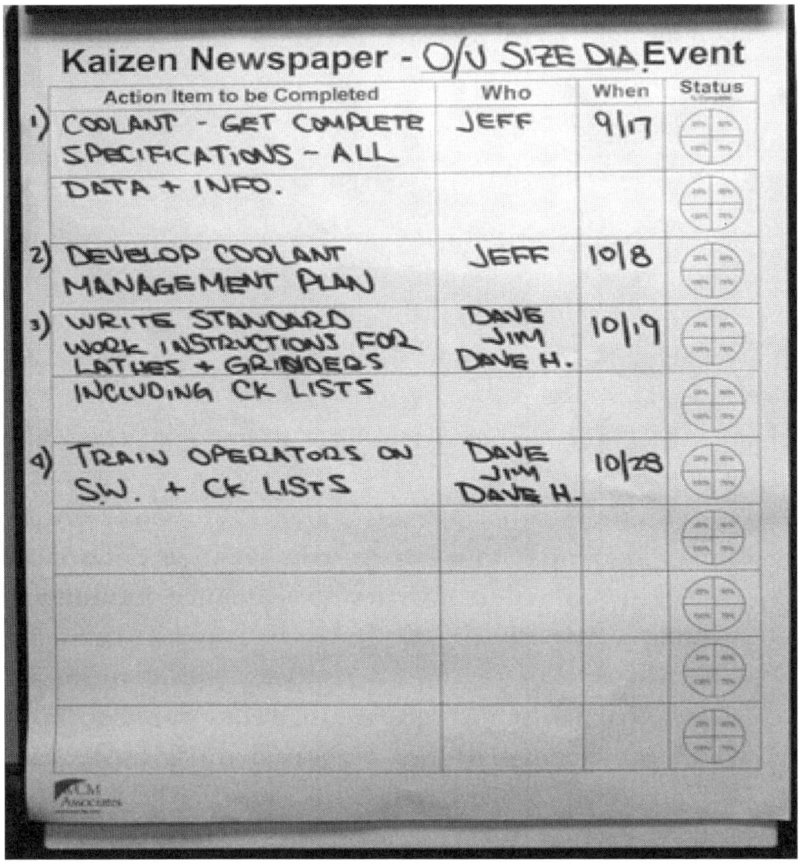

Figure #52
Countermeasures Kaizen Newspaper

√ *Step 9*

Once the action plan is complete and there is consensus by the team that the plan will achieve the desired results, it is time to start implementing the plan. The team plans its work and works its plan. Everyone on the team must be committed to the implementation and hold themselves accountable and responsible for the results.

One tool that truly bridges the gap between the "improve" part of structured problem solving and the "control" phase of problem solving is Error Proofing/Mistake Proofing. Error Proofing is built on the following philosophy:

- The goal is to prevent defects—not detect them!

- The simplest, and often most inexpensive, methods are best

- Machines and processes occasionally fail and make errors

- Human error is not only possible—but inevitable!

There are eight principles of Error Proofing/Mistake Proofing:

1. Build quality into processes—make it impossible to turn out defective items even if a mistake is made.

2. All inadvertent errors and defects can be eliminated. Recognize that defects are not inevitable.

3. Stop doing it wrong and start doing it right—now!

4. Don't think up excuses—think about how to do it right.

5. A 60% chance of success is good enough. Don't wait for the home run idea, that may never come!

6. Mistakes and defects can be reduced to zero when we all work together to eliminate them.

7. Ten heads are better than one—get the "Team" focused on improvement ideas.

8. Get to the root cause, using the 5 Why's. Ask Why five times, and only then ask, "How do we fix it?"

The team should take the time to brainstorm ideas on how to implement Error Proofing into every process. This should become a part of an organization's culture.

Control

There are always several things that must occur at the last step of structured problem solving regardless of the corrective action taken. Whenever we talk about corrective action, we are speaking about process or procedural changes. All process changes must be documented in the Standard Work Instructions and Visual Controls. People working in the process must be made aware of procedural changes and educated to the new process.

The next part of "control" is to ensure that the necessary metrics are in place to monitor progress, or demonstrate improvement, toward the goal. Remember the sign that is kept on my desk, "In God we trust, valid data required by everyone else."

√ Step 9

A completed example of a Countermeasures chart is shown on page 189.

TEAM ACTION FOR STEP 9:

Load the Excel spreadsheet from the enclosed CD onto your computer. Click on the label marked "Countermeasures". Use the Countermeasures format for any items that turn RED on the Lean Implementation Plan (Step 7) or the Bowling Chart (Step 8).

EXAMPLE

Countermeasure Sheet

Date:

Define

Problem statement: Returns from customers are running above our 3% of sales target

Goal for the team: Reduce returns to less than 1% of sales

Measure

Run chart:

Pareto analysis

Analyze

Fishbone diagram: [top 3 issues]

Quantities incorrect
Wrong color
Duplicate order

5 Why's: [Quantities incorrect]

Typed incorrect quantities into the system
Was in a hurry
Near the end of the day
Tired
Was not able to take a break

Improve

Results of brainstorming:

Rotate order entry people every hour to allow for breaks
Error proof computer screens so as to be able to select from a range of colors

Control

Action Plan:

What	Who	When
Set up rotation schedule for order entry personnel	LR	End of Q1
Make modifications to computer program for order entry quantities & colors	MW	End of Q1
Rewrite order entry procedures and train all personnel	MW	End of Q1
Communicate all procedural changes & audit process	AL	End of Q1
Continue to measure & monitor process	TD	End of Q1

What Error Proofing devices have you implemented to prevent recuring problems?

Brainstorming: (# 1–49)

Step 10:

Conducting Monthly Business Reviews

STEP 10 OBJECTIVE

Conduct Monthly Business Review meetings to reiterate that the implementation activities are on target to support achievement of the organization's goals.

This is a review session of the Bowling Chart (Step 8), not a problem solving meeting.

√ *Step 10*

10 Steps to Successful Policy Deployment

1. Establish a Mission and Guiding Principles

2. Develop Business Goals

3. Brainstorm for Opportunities to Achieve Goals

4. Define Parameters to Value Opportunities

5. Establish Weighting Requirements, Rate Opportunities, and Prioritize

6. Conduct a Reality Check

7. Develop Lean Implementation Plan

8. Develop Bowling Chart

9. Countermeasures

10. **Conducting Business Reviews**

The sole purpose of the Monthly Business Review meeting is for the members of the organization to update the Bowling Chart for the Leadership Team. The Review is not designed to do structured problem solving or to fill out a countermeasures sheet. The people accountable (as identified in Step 7), the owner (as identified in Step 8), or the appropriate team decides how they will review and react to the metrics going "red." In the Monthly Business Review, the owner, person accountable, or the team reports that they are either "on track" or "X days/weeks behind." See Script A and Script B on page 193. If individuals or teams come to the review unprepared to do an update, then the Leadership Team must look at how the organization's "system" (for which management is responsible) allows this to happen. The usual suspects, in order of most to least probable, are:

♦ The team does not feel empowered

♦ The team is not given time to do structured problem solving (usually by a supervisor who does not support this activity)

♦ Members are new to teams and need the support of the organization's Lean Facilitator

Business Review meetings must be held monthly like clockwork.

If good visual measurements and visual systems are in the workplace areas for the required activities of Step 7 and the goals of Step 8, then none of the Monthly Business Review updates should be a surprise. Remember, good visuals mean that anyone should be able to walk through the organization and understand how everyone is progressing against their goals without asking a question. Any surprises that do occur should be handled on a Kaizen Newspaper with immediate assignments to "Who" and "When." This Kaizen Newspaper then becomes part of the monthly review.

Conducting business reviews should be relatively simple. If this process is used religiously, people will come to monthly meetings prepared to present one of two scripts. Script "A" would indicate that a project metric is on track and is expected to stay on track.

SCRIPT A:

- It's on Track,

- It'll Stay on Track,

- Any questions?

Script "B" would indicate that things are not necessarily going as planned. However, it means that the individual or team responsible for this project metric is monitoring it on a daily basis and using structured problem solving to put a plan in place to correct the situation.

SCRIPT B:

- It's "X" Weeks Behind,

- The Cause is "Y",

- The Impact is "Z",

- Here's How & When We'll Catch Up

- Any questions?

√ **Step 10**

The Bowling Chart should be referenced in the monthly all associates meetings. These meetings are a signature activity of World Class Enterprises. This gives everyone an update of how the company is doing against the goals. For this reason, the Bowling Chart review meeting should be held a couple of days before the monthly all associate meeting. When not being updated or referenced, the Bowling Chart (a roll size version), should be posted in a very visible part(s) of the organization.

A recommended agenda for your Monthly Business Reviews should include most or all of the following (see Figure #54 also):

1. Start by reviewing the organization's Mission and Guiding Principles. It is not uncommon for a World Class Enterprise to review its financials at this time. Take the time to review the Income Statement and Balance Sheet. This helps set the tone and begins to challenge the team if the Lean improvement initiatives are not achieving the business goals of the organization. For example, if all the Lean initiatives are "On Track" and everyone believes they will stay on track, but the organization is losing money, something is wrong! We either did not do a good job of identifying the greatest opportunities in the organization or maybe there is a change in market conditions (environmental factors).

If this is the case, we may need to ask ourselves if we should make changes to the plan. Policy Deployment is a dynamic process and can be changed during the year. It should only be changed, however, when it no longer reflects strategic priorities for the business due to the emergence of:

- Compelling business issues

- Important market or competitor intelligence

- Improvement priorities completed or ineffective

"Unachievable Goals" do not justify changes to the plan and any changes to the plan must be approved by the entire Leadership Team.

30 minutes

2. Review Kaizen Newspaper from the last monthly Business Review (if a newspaper has been started). This ensures all Kaizen Newspaper action items are complete and/or updated.

5 minutes per item

3. Review status of the organization's goals (only) on the Bowling Chart

15 minutes

4. Review the Bowling Chart and Key Performance Indicators. Focus on any items that have turned RED. Ensure that countermeasures are in place for RED items and that these countermeasures have been Error Proofed.

10 minutes per RED item

5. Review the Lean and Safety Implementation Plans (Step 7). Focus on any items that have turned RED. Ensure that countermeasures are in place for RED items and that these countermeasures have been Error Proofed. Review the results of any Kaizen Events with the team (it is always a good idea to invite one of the teams to do a "report out" at the monthly company meeting also).

√ *Step 10*

During this meeting, the Leadership Team should note the growth of the organization in several key areas:

♦ Developing and implementing the Lean Plan

♦ The level of understanding of the Lean Concepts

♦ The effective use of the Lean Tools

♦ The beginning development of a Lean Culture

30 minutes for the Step 7 plan
15 minutes per Kaizen Event team

6. Set agenda, date, and time for next meeting
5 minutes

As you can see, the meeting is used as a review meeting. The Leadership team should not be problem solving in this meeting. Problem solving is the responsibility of the people on the Implementation and Kaizen Teams. They are the experts.

At the end of the Monthly Business Review meeting it is a good idea to check the effectiveness of your team. The "Learning Cycle Checklist" (see Figure #53) is a good tool to audit and to use to continuously improve the team's effectiveness. It is a simple tool; all you have to do is go around the room and have everyone score each category (Setting Goals, Assigning Accountability, Handling Conflict, Making Decisions, Meeting Effectively, Learning/Feedback, and Collaborating with Other Groups) on a scale from 1 to 5 (1 = poor to 5 = World Class). If the team ends up with a low score in one particular category, it then can brainstorm what the team may do the next time it meets to improve the overall effectiveness of the team.

For example; let's say the team awards itself a low score on "Meeting Effectiveness" because meetings do not start and end on time. The team may use structured problem solving and conclude that the reason meetings do not start on time is because people arrive late to the meeting. The team may then conduct a brainstorming session to establish consensus on how to improve on-time attendance to the meeting. If action items are required, these actions are added to the Kaizen Newspaper.

An example of a filled out Bowling Chart ready for a Monthly Business Review meeting is shown on page 200.

√ *Step 10*

Using Learning Cycle Criteria in Teams

Setting Goals	• Is there a discussion of goals involving the whole team? • Is there agreement and commitment to team goals? • Are differences in members' understanding of the goals discussed and resolved? • Are goals and plans recorded so that they are clear to all?
Assigning Accountability	• Is there a clear understanding about who is to do what and when? • Are there tracking measures in place so that the team can ensure that work is completed effectively? • Are roles allocated to take advantage of members' interests and capabilities? • Are changes made in role assignments to improve the team's ability to achieve goals?
Handling Conflict	• Do people openly and spontaneously bring up differences of opinion? • Do individuals handle conflicts constructively as a creative tool? • Do people use inquiry to gain further understanding about others' views? • Do people provide reasons for their opinions?
Making Decisions	• Are decisions made on time? • Are decisions based on business reasons and data? • Are decisions made by consensus with a focus on the best solution for everyone? • Is everyone in the team involved in the decision-making process or, at least, fully committed to the decision made? • Are important decisions revised based on new information?
Meeting Effectively	• Is time managed well during the team exercise? • Are priorities set so that key issues are addressed first? • Are there contingency plans for reallocating priorities when time is tight? • Do people use LearningCycle ✓'s and ground rules to improve the meeting's efficiency? • Do meetings start and stop exactly on time?
Learning / Feedback	• Are LearningCycle ✓'s used regularly? • Are suggestions made at the beginning of the activity or project? • Do people comment freely during the activity in order to suggest improvements? • Is time set aside for "post" checks at the end of every meeting or activity? • Do all members contribute to LearningCycle ✓'s?
Collaborating with Other Groups	• Are people in this group listening and seeking out input from other groups? • Do people in this group make an effort to understand the goals of the other groups while avoiding unconstructive attitudes? • Do members seek and communicate common goals with other groups? • Does this group present a united and productive image?

Figure #53
Learning Cycle Checklist

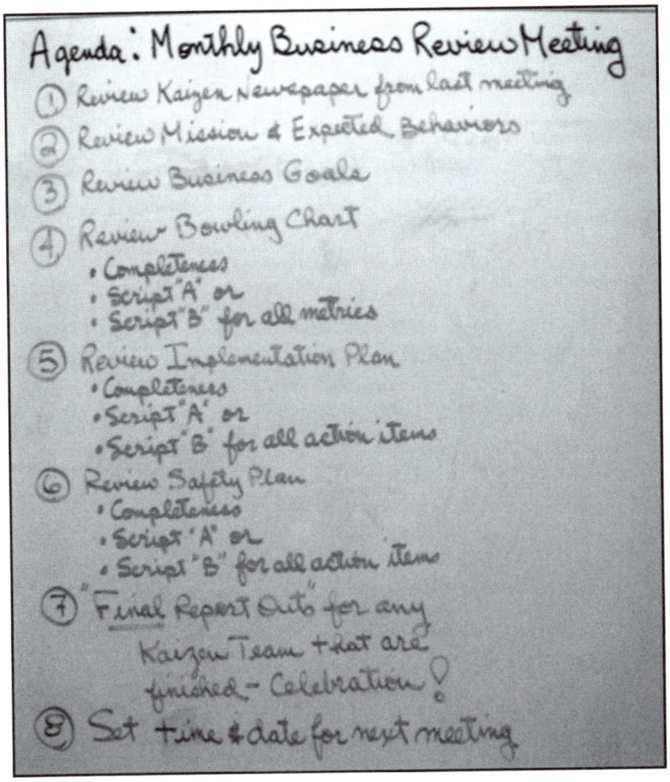

Conducting Monthly Business Reviews

Figure #54

TEAM ACTION FOR STEP 10:

Load the Excel spreadsheet from the enclosed CD onto your computer. Click on the label marked "Bowling Chart". Update the Bowling Chart and then the Lean Implementation Plan with the new information supplied by the individuals and teams. Create new posters/charts for the organization's visual management system to make sure everyone in the organization can see the latest updates.

√ Step 10

EXAMPLE

#	High-Level Business Goals & Key Performance Indicators (KPIs)	Owner	JOP	YTD		Jan	Feb	Mar
	High-Level Business Goals							
1	Achieve ZERO lost injury days for the next 12 months	MW	5	0	Plan	0	0	0
				0	Act	0	0	0
2	Improve Net Income from 3% to 8% of sales by the end of the fiscal year	LR	3.0%	3.0%	Plan	3.0%	3.0%	3.0%
				2.8%	Act	3.0%	3.2%	2.2%
3	Improve Free Cash Flow from 30% of net income to 70% of net income by the end of the fiscal year	VF	30.0%	30%	Plan	30%	30%	30%
				34%	Act	31%	34%	37%
4	Increase Revenue from $32 million to $36 million without eroding profits by the end of the fiscal year	LR	$32 M	$7.8	Plan	$2.6	$2.6	$2.6
				$8.1	Act	$2.6	$2.7	$2.8
	Key Performance Indicators (KPIs)							
5	Reduce System Cycle Time (from quote to cash) from 67 days to 30 days by the end of Q1	LR	67 days	54 days	Plan	67 days	50 days	45 days
				51 days	Act	67 days	47 days	40 days
6	Reduce returns from 3% of sales to less than 1% of sales by the end of Q1	VF	3.0%	3.0%	Plan	3.0%	3.0%	3.0%
				3.4%	Act	3.2%	3.0%	4.0%
7	Reduce scrap in the foundry from 6% to 3% of sales by the end of Q1	MW	6.0%	6.0%	Plan	6.0%	6.0%	6.0%
				5.8%	Act	5.8%	5.6%	6.0%
8	Reduce set-up time on machine #4 from 3 hours to less than 30 minutes by the end of Q2	TD	180 min	180	Plan	180	180	180
				180	Act	180	170	190
9	Reduce finished goods inventory from $9 million to less than $3 million by the end of Q2	PL	$9M	$8.67	Plan	$9.00	$9.00	$8.00
				$8.50	Act	$9.00	$8.50	$8.00
10	Consolidate warehouses after reducing finished goods inventory by the end of Q3 -- potential cost saving of $800K	PL	Project	$0.0	Plan	$0.0	$0.0	$0.0
				$0.0	Act	$0.0	$0.0	$0.0
11	Reduce pricing errors from 9 per order to zero by the end of Q3	LR	9	9	Plan	9	9	9
				7	Act	9	7	5
12	Reduce turnover of key personnel from 3% to zero by the end of Q4	AL	3.0%	3.0%	Plan	3.0%	3.0%	3.0%
				2.1%	Act	3.6%	0.0%	2.8%
13	Develop a process to respond to an RFQ in a single phone call by the end of Q4	MW	3 Days	3 Days	Plan	3 Days	3 Days	3 Days
				3 Days	Act	3 Days	3 Days	3 Days

☐ = Project is at or above goal (Script A)
■ = Project is "RED" (below goal) and requires a countermeasure (Script B)

200

Conclusion/Summary

Lean eliminates waste to improve the flow of information and material so an organization can meet its business goals and objectives. Many organizations fail to understand that there should be a direct link between the implementation of Lean and the company's financials. Lean is designed to improve safety, profitability, cash flow, and revenue. In fact, if management does not see a clear link between the implementation of Lean and the business objectives of an organization, the Lean initiative will be implemented as an appendage and will fail.

Larry Rubrich cites the top 10 reasons why lean implementations fail in his book, *How to Prevent Lean Implementation Failures, 10 Reasons Why Failures Occur*:

1. Lack of top-down leadership and management support

2. Lack of communication

3. Lack of middle management/supervisor buy-in

√ *Conclusion/Summary*

4. Not understanding that this is about developing your people

5. Lack of customer focus

6. Lack of improvement measurements

7. Lack of Lean leadership

8. People measures/goals which are not aligned with implementation goals

9. Using Kaizen Events as the sole improvement mechanism

10. Improperly designed bonus systems—bonus pay systems where the only measure is company profitability

The number one reason that Lean initiatives fail is the lack of top-down leadership and management support, but ultimately all 10 reasons are about failures at the Leadership Team level—the failure of the Leadership Team to get everyone in the organization pulling in the direction of the Leadership Team's vision and goals. Experience shows that 98% of the people in organizations want to take care of the customer, want the company to be successful, and want to have a job with the organization in the future. What's missing in unsuccessful organizations is Leadership.

Philip Crosby, who wrote such great books as *Quality is Free*, and *Quality Without Tears*, often said that management has a choice. They can choose between ballet or hockey style management. Ballet style management is where everyone in the ballet knows what is going to happen two minutes into the second act so that they can practice. The stage crew builds the set, the orchestra practices their music, the actors rehearse the scene, and they all know that two minutes into the scene, the music is going to start playing and Ivanoff is going to pick up Natasha and put her into the swan boat and the lights are going to change. That is ballet, where everyone knows what is going to happen and they can help one another.

The only other choice you have is hockey style management. Hockey is a great game but no one knows what is going to happen two minutes into the second period, so we cannot rehearse or practice what is suppose to happen. In hockey style management, everyone knows their place in the organization, everyone has their uniform and at 8:00 a.m. someone drops the puck and everyone runs around all day chasing the puck. Then we all fall exhausted into our chairs at the end of the day not realizing that we have just solved the same problem over again for the umpteenth time.

So management has a choice. They can choose between ballet or hockey style management. Using the information in this workbook, management can orchestrate a successful Deployment of their Policies, using a Lean Implementation Plan, throughout their organization.

Appendix A

Advanced Lean Tools

As mentioned in the Lean Tools summary, there are two additional Advanced Lean Tools that organizations deploy once they have a firm foundation in the standard Lean Tools and the organization is all pulling in the same direction. Jumping to these powerful tools without teamwork and a Lean foundation in place will be a frustrating failure.

3P (Production Preparation Planning)

Lean experts typically view 3P as one of the most powerful waste eliminating and transformative advanced manufacturing tools. Whereas normal Kaizen Events and other Lean methods take a production process as a given and seek to make improvements, the Production Preparation Process (3P) focuses on eliminating waste through product and process design. 3P represents the ultimate use of the Kaizen Event, the Pre-Production Kaizen Event. Any type of improvement made at this point in the product and process design is easier and can be done at a much lower cost then when the product is in production.

√ *Appendix A*

3P seeks to meet customer requirements by starting with a clean product-development slate to rapidly create and test potential product and process designs that require the least time, material, and capital resources. This method typically involves a diverse group of individuals in a multi-day creative process to identify several alternative ways to meet the customer's needs using different product or process designs. 3P can also design production processes that eliminate multiple process steps and that utilize homemade, right-sized equipment that better meet production needs.

Ultimately, 3P methods represent a dramatic shift from the continuous, incremental improvement of existing processes sought with normal Kaizen Events. Instead, 3P offers potential to make "quantum leap" design improvements that can improve performance and eliminate waste to a level beyond that which can be achieved through the continual improvement of existing processes.

With 3P, the teams spend several days in this Pre-Production Kaizen Event (with singular focus on a 3P activity) working to develop multiple alternatives for each process step and evaluating each alternative against manufacturing criteria (e.g., designated takt time) and a preferred cost. The goal is typically to develop a process or product design that meets customer requirements best in the "least waste way."

Often, 3P activities are given their own area/space in the organization since some 3P activities (the redesign of an existing product) may take several months and may be the focus of numerous Pre-Production Kaizen Events. Figures #55 and 56 are examples of 3P activities where cardboard and then wood design mock-ups were made before the design was moved forward.

3P is very effective in reducing manufacturing, processing, and assembly costs since these costs usually are born in the early design phase of the project. Many different studies have found that as much as 80% of a new product's cost is set in concrete at the first drawing release phase of the product. Unfortunately, many organizations find it difficult to implement changes to their new product development process since it is currently done in an uncollaborative environment.

**Figure #55
Small Cardboard and Wood Assembly
Mock-ups of a Vehicle Cab**

√ Appendix A

**Figure #56
Full Scale Wood Mock-up**

DFMA (Design for Manufacturability and Assembly)

Designing for Manufacturing and Assembly (DFMA) is a technique for reducing the cost of a product by breaking the product down into its simplest components. All members of the design team can understand the product's assembly sequence and material flow early in the design process.

DFMA tools lead the development team to reduce the number of individual parts that make up the product and ensure that any additional or remaining parts are easy to handle and insert during the assembly process. DFMA encourages the integration of parts and processes, which helps reduce the amount of assembly labor and cost. DFMA efforts include programs to minimize the time it takes for the total product development cycle, manufacturing cycle, and product life-cycle costs. DFMA design programs also promote team cooperation, supplier strategy, and business considerations at an early stage in the product development process.

DFMA considerations include:

- Minimize number of parts

- Minimize number of special or unique parts

- Assembly sequence restrictions

- Common components across a product family

Additionally, Error Proofing should be integrated into the DFMA process so that parts are designed so they can be assembled only one way—the correct way. Tooling and fixturing should be designed to double check that the previous operations were done correctly (Error Proofing—detection at downstream station).

The DFMA process is composed of two major components: design for assembly (DFA) and design for manufacturing (DFM). DFA is the labor side of the product cost. This is the labor needed to transform the new design into a customer-ready product. DFM is the material and tooling side of the new product. DFM breaks the parts fabrication process down into its simplest steps, such as the type of equipment used to produce the part, and the fabrication cycle time to produce the part, and then calculates a cost for each functional step in the process. The program team should use the DFM tools to establish the material target cost before the new product design effort starts.

The ultimate goal of DFMA is to make it "impossible" to make it or assemble it incorrectly.

Index

Symbols

3P Process 50, 205–207
5 Whys 181–182
5S 28–29, 36

A

Added Value Percentage
   Calculation 31–32
Adding Value 7–8
   Definition 26
   Manufacturing Definition 7
Administration
   Information Product 7–8, 33
   Process Cell 33–35
   Productivity 8
Armstrong, Neil 170
Ayers, Robert 83

B

Behavioral Expectations 60–63, 88–99
   Examples 95–99
Benefit and Effort
   Using for Prioritization 128–129
   Weighting 128–135
Berry, Tim 80
Bowling Chart 157–167, 170–171, 191–200
   Accountability 162, 174
Brainstorming 17–18, 112–119, 179–185
   Affinitizing 115–116
   Rules 112–114, 183–184
   Voting to Prioritize 116–119, 181
Business Goals
   Breakthrough Goals and Objectives 105, 164
   High Level 103–104, 109, 144, 158
   SMART 101, 104, 109, 160

C

Cash Flow 15
Cause and Effect Diagram. *See* Fishbone Diagram
Change
   And Human Nature 69–71
   Implementation Prerequisites 21–22
Communication 68–71. *See also* Visual
   Management
   Lack of 69–71
Covey, Steven 82
Crosby, Philip 202–203
Culture
   Acquiring 52
   Corporate 54–57
   Definition 52
   Leadership Accountability 59–65
   Reason for 53–54

D

Daily Management 105–108, 164
Deming, W. Edwards
   14 Points 97–98
Departmentalization 8–10
DFMA 50, 208–209

E

Empowerment 72
Error Proofing 38–41, 186–187

F

Facilitator
   Kaizen Events 46–47
   Need for 10, 138
Fishbone Diagram 102–103, 179–181
Force Field Analysis 150

G

General Electric 88–89
Genie Industries 96
Guiding Principles and Behavioral Expectations 88–99

√ Index

H

Hanks, Tom 170
Harris, Ed 170
Hockey Style Management 202–203
Hoshin Kanri 10
How to Prevent Lean Implementation Failures 3, 60, 112, 139, 201

I

Idea Benefit 121–125
Idea Effort 121–125
Idea Prioritization 131–135, 138
Idea Valuations 121–125
Industry Week 1
Inspection 38–41
Ishikawa Diagram. *See* Fishbone Diagram
ITT Industries 83, 87, 139

K

Kaizen
   Definition 46–47
   Newspaper 114–115, 185, 193
   Team Formation 46
Kaizen Event 19, 46–47, 202
   And Daily Management 108
   Report Out 69
   Visibility 49
Kanbans 36–37
   Waste Elimination by 37
Kennedy, John F.
   President 80–81
Key Performance Indicators (KPIs) 144, 160–162, 171
Kotter, John P. 21, 80
Kranz, Gene 170

L

Leadership 59–71
   Four Absolutes of 65–67
   Visionary 80, 83
Leadership Team 4–5, 171
   And Culture Change 59–71, 93
   And Teamwork 68–75

Definition 5
Goal Setting 15–18, 101–109
Honesty Requirement 71
Lean
   Percent Utilized 2
   Concepts 23–26
   Culture 12–14, 51–58
   Enabler Activities 143, 145–149
   Four Components of 11–14 76–77, 146
   Planning 11, 14–23
   Toolbox 27
   Tools 11, 12, 27–50
      Impact 48
   Tools Summary 47–48
Lean Implementation Plan 143–155
   Accountability 151, 174
Lean Sigma 27
   Goal 38
   Problem Solving 37–38
      Analyze 179–182
      Control 187
      Define 175–178
      DMAIC 164, 171–189
      Improve 183–184
      Measure 178
      Pitfalls 173
      Root Cause 181–182
Lean System Thinking 5, 74
Learning Cycle Checklist 196–198
Lovell, Jim 170

M

Meetings
   Company 194
Mission Statement 80–87
   Guidelines 80–84
   Reason for 80–81
Mistake Proofing 38–41, 186–187
Monthly Business Reviews 171, 191–200
   Agenda 194–199

P

Policy Deployment 1–10
Process Cells 33–35
   Waste Elimination in 34–35

R

RACI 151–153
Reality Check 18, 137–141
Rubrich, Larry 3, 28, 81, 139, 201
Rumors
   Why They Exist 69–71
Ryan, Dick 61

S

Safety 16–17, 114
Script A 192–193
Script B 192–193
Set-up Reduction 35–36
   Waste Elimination by 35–36
Sherman, Stratford 88
SIPOC 176–177
Solomon, Jerrold 130
Spaghetti Diagrams 41–42
St. Camillus 87, 95
Step 1 79–99
   Objective 79
Step 10 191–200
   Objective 191
Step 2 101–109
   Objective 101
Step 3 111–120
   Objective 111
Step 4 121–125
   Objective 121
Step 5 127–135
   Objective 127
Step 6 137–141
   Objective 137
Step 7 143–155
   Objective 143
Step 8 157–167
   Objective 157
Step 9 169–189

   Objective 169
SWOT Analysis and Core Competencies 84–87, 119
System Cycle Time 29–32, 35

T

Takt Time
   Calculation 31–32
   Definition 31
Taylor, Fredrick W. 55–56, 59
Team
   Definition 5
   Playbook 68
Teamwork 73–75
   BEEC Factor in Problem Solving 73
   Requirements for 43, 68
Tichy, Noel 88
Total Productive Maintenance 32–33
   OEE Measurement 33
Toyota 41

V

Valuation Parameters 121–125
Value Stream Mapping 29–32
   Administrative Lead-Times 7
   Four Step Process 30–31
Value Streams 75
Vision 21–22, 80–83
Visual Management 43–45

W

Waste
   8 Types 24–26
   Definition 24–26
Watson, Mattie 28
Welch, Jack 88–93
Wiremold Company 61–64